SHARE THE DREAM

Shining a Light in a Divided World
through Six Principles of

MARTIN LUTHER KING JR.

BIBLE STUDY GUIDE | SIX SESSIONS

MATTHEW DANIELS AND CHRIS BROUSSARD

WITH KATARA PATTON

HarperChristian
Resources

CONTENTS

"I Have a Dream" v

How to Use This Guide ix

SESSION 1: LOVE 1

SESSION 2: CONSCIENCE 21

SESSION 3: JUSTICE 43

SESSION 4: FREEDOM 65

SESSION 5: PERSEVERANCE 85

SESSION 6: HOPE 105

Leader's Guide 125

About the Authors 129

Endnotes 131

"I HAVE A DREAM"

Let justice roll on like a river, righteousness like a never-failing stream.

Amos 5:24

THE DATE WAS AUGUST 28, 1963. The place was Washington, DC. A crowd of more than 250,000 civil rights supporters had gathered outside the Lincoln Memorial, filling the area around the reflecting pool and out toward the Washington Monument, to take part in the March on Washington for Jobs and Freedom. The march was partly intended to demonstrate support for civil rights legislation proposed by President John F. Kennedy. The speakers had agreed to keep their speeches calm so as not to overly incite the crowd that had gathered.[1]

One of the speakers that day was Dr. Martin Luther King Jr., a Baptist minister who had been thrust into the limelight as a result of his leadership in the civil rights movement. Dr. King had designed his speech as an homage to Abraham Lincoln's Gettysburg Address, but he departed from his prepared script when Mahalia Jackson, a gospel singer who was also performing that day, called out, "Tell them about the dream, Martin!"[2] What followed was the now famous "I Have a Dream" speech, in which Dr. King outlined his vision of freedom and equality in a land that still practiced racism and hatred.[3]

As one historian noted, "With a single phrase, King joined Jefferson and Lincoln in the ranks of men who've shaped modern America."[4] Dr. King, and other courageous men and women of his day, were able to change history through the power of a dream rooted not only in human principles but also in God's love for *all* humanity. In other words, there was a *spiritual* dimension to the early civil rights movement. This becomes especially evident when you learn the spiritual backstory of what Dr. King and others were able to achieve.

Ambassador Andrew Young, one of Dr. King's closest confidants in the civil rights movement, stated they were only able to overcome the incredible violence, threats, and legal and political opposition that they faced on all sides "by the power of the Spirit." He went on to explain, "We would be planning to go to Place A for a rally. But someone would have a dream the night before telling us to go to Place B. So, in obedience to the dream, we would go to Place B. And there would be a bomb at Place A that would have taken out the whole civil rights movement in its infancy. When that happens to you . . . you learn to be led by the Spirit."

In many ways, this sounds like a description of the early church. In spite of the violence and persecution they faced, "those who had been scattered preached the word wherever they went" (Acts 8:4). The first believers were led by the Spirit, and as a result, the church continued to grow day by day. Ultimately, Christianity transformed the Roman Empire itself.

Most of us today would agree that we need that *same* power to overcome the growing darkness and violence in our world. We need the Holy Spirit to guide us, work through us, and empower us to transform our communities, cities, and nations for Christ. We need to be active in partnering with the Spirit's work to *share the dream* today.

Throughout Dr. King's life—and in the last public speech he gave before he was assassinated—he used the parable of the good Samaritan as an illustration of the love, mercy, and compassion of God being extended across the boundaries of race and culture. You might recall that Jesus told the parable in response to a religious teacher's question, "Who is my neighbor?" (Luke 10:29). Many people, both in that time and still today, prefer to define *neighbor* as narrowly as possible. But Dr. King noted the following about Jesus' response:

> Jesus immediately pulled that question from mid-air, and placed it on a dangerous curve between Jerusalem and Jericho. And he talked about a certain man, who fell among thieves. You remember that a Levite and a priest passed by on the other side. They didn't stop to help him. And finally a man of another race came by. He got down from his beast, decided not to be compassionate by proxy. But with him, administered first aid, and helped the man in need. Jesus ended up saying, this was the good man, this was the great man, because he had the capacity to project the "I" into the "thou," and to be concerned about his brother.[5]

We live in a world that is divided. It's all too easy for us to focus on our differences and "pass to the other side" instead of bridging the gap. But Jesus calls us to be like the Samaritan in the parable who possessed a "universal altruism." We are to build networks and relationships that represent the antidote to the world's ideologies of hatred, racism, and violence. We are called to be a people who understand, live, experience, and ultimately form a community around the unifying principles at the heart of the dream to which Dr. King dedicated his life.

This is why we created the *Share the Dream* curriculum. We hope that you will join us in exploring how *you* can participate in sharing Dr. King's dream in our time.

HOW TO USE THIS GUIDE

Dr. King once wrote, "I am convinced that the universe is under the control of a loving purpose, and that in the struggle for righteousness man has cosmic companionship. Behind the harsh appearances of the world there is a benign power."[6] Dr. King embraced this belief in a benign power—in a loving God who was sovereign over the affairs of this earth—in spite of the incredible challenges, hostilities, adversities, and persecution that he faced on a daily basis.

In this study, you will look at six biblical principles that shaped Dr. Martin Luther King Jr.'s belief in an all-loving and all-powerful God, compelled him to act on behalf of those who were oppressed, and empowered him to stand for justice in a very unjust world. The legacy that Dr. King left behind has literally changed our history. You have the power to do the same if you are willing to embrace these same transcendent principles in your world today.

Before you begin this study, keep in mind that there are a few ways you can go through the material. You can experience the study with others in a small group (such as a Bible study, Sunday school class, or home group), or you may choose to go through the content on your own. Either way, the videos for each session are available for you to view at any time via streaming (see the instructions provided with this guide).

GROUP STUDY

Each session in this study is divided into two parts: (1) a group study section and (2) a personal study section. The group study section provides a basic framework on how to open your time together, get the most out of the video content, and discuss the key ideas that were presented in the teaching. Each session includes the following:

- **Welcome:** A short note about the topic of the session for you to read on your own before you meet as a group.
- **Connect:** A few icebreaker questions to get you and your group members thinking about the topic and interacting with each other.
- **Watch:** An outline of the key points covered in each video teaching along with space for you to take notes as you watch each session.

- **Discuss:** Questions to help you and your group reflect on the teaching material presented and apply it to your lives.
- **Respond:** A short personal exercise to help reinforce the key ideas.
- **Pray:** A place for you to record prayer requests and praises for the week.

If you are doing this study in a group, have your own copy of the study guide so you can write down your thoughts, responses, and reflections—and so you will have access to the videos via streaming. Finally, keep these points in mind:

- **Facilitation:** If you are doing this study in a group, you will want to appoint someone to serve as a facilitator. This person will be responsible for starting the video and keeping track of time during discussions and activities. If *you* have been chosen for this role, there are some resources in the back of this guide that can help you lead your group through the study.

- **Faithfulness:** Your group is a place where tremendous growth can happen as you reflect on the Bible, ask questions, and learn what God is doing in other people's lives. For this reason, be fully committed and attend each session so you can build trust and rapport with the other members.

- **Friendship:** The goal of any small group is to serve as a place where people can share, learn about God, and build friendships. So make your group a safe place. Be honest about your thoughts and feelings, but also listen carefully to everyone else in the group. Keep anything personal that your group members share in confidence so that you can create an authentic community where people can heal, be challenged, and grow spiritually.

If you are going through this study on your own, read the opening Welcome section and reflect on the questions in the Connect section. Watch the video and use the prompts that have been provided to take notes. Finally, personalize the questions and exercises in the Discuss and Respond sections. Close by recording any requests you want to pray about during the week.

PERSONAL STUDY

The personal study is for you to work through on your own during the week. Each exercise is designed to help you explore the key ideas you uncovered during your group time and delve into passages of Scripture that will help you apply those principles to your life. Go at your own pace, doing a little each day—or tackle the material all at once. Remember to spend a few moments in silence and in prayer each day to listen to what God might be saying to you.

Each section contains three personal studies that open with a brief devotion for you to read, a few passages for you to read or look up, and several reflection questions to help you apply the truths of God's Word to your life. Following this, there is a Connect & Catch Up page with questions for you to answer with a friend, either over a phone call or a cup of coffee, and to finish any personal studies that you didn't have a chance to complete during the week.

Note that if you are doing this study as part of a group, and are unable to finish (or even start) these personal studies for the week, you should still attend the group time. Be assured that you are wanted and welcome even if you don't have your "homework" done. The group studies and personal studies are intended to help you hear what God wants you to hear and apply what he is saying to your life. So, as you go through the *Share the Dream* study on the life and teachings of Dr. Martin Luther King Jr., be listening for the Lord to speak to you.

LOVE

Whoever does not love does not know God, because God is love.

1 JOHN 4:8

"Even though we face the **difficulties** of today and tomorrow . . . I still have a **dream**."

DR. MARTIN LUTHER KING JR.

WELCOME |

On April 3, 1963, just a few months before delivering his "I Have a Dream" speech, Dr. King led a series of protests against segregation in Birmingham, Alabama. One week later, on April 12, the authorities imprisoned Dr. King and many of his fellow activists for their actions. While in jail, Dr. King learned of a public statement made by eight white clergymen that appealed to the local black population to use the courts to air their grievances and not take to the streets.

The clergyman counseled "law and order and common sense" and not the "extremist" actions that Dr. King was taking.[7] In response, and while still in jail, Dr. King penned a letter in which he said, "I must admit that I was initially disappointed in being so categorized. But as I continued to think about the matter I gradually gained a bit of satisfaction from being considered an extremist. Was not Jesus an extremist in love—'Love your enemies, bless them that curse you, pray for them that despitefully use you.'"[8]

We use the word *love* today to mean many things. We throw it around to express how we feel about a food or an event. We use it to describe the good feelings we have about others. *Love* is an ambiguous and overused word. But the type of love that Jesus calls us to have for others is active and sacrificial. It was this kind of love that enabled Dr. King and others in the civil rights movement to see those who were persecuting them as children of God and love them in spite of the evil acts they were perpetrating.

In this first session, we will take a closer look at the power of this kind of love and explore how those who embrace it—like Dr. King—can change their world for Christ.

CONNECT | 15 MINUTES

If any of your group members don't know each other, take a few minutes to introduce yourselves. Then, to get things started, discuss one of the following questions:

- What is your primary goal or hope for participating in this study?

  — *or* —

- What is one thing you know about Dr. Martin Luther King Jr.? What is one thing that you would like to know more about him?

WATCH | 20 MINUTES

Watch the video, which you can access by playing the DVD or through streaming (see the instructions provided with this guide). Use the following outline to record any thoughts or concepts that stand out to you.

OUTLINE

 I. Dr. Martin Luther King Jr. described himself as an "extremist for love."
  A. Dr. King stated that he was following the example of Jesus, who was also an extremist for love.
  B. He noted that an extremist for love follows Jesus' command to "love your enemies and pray for those who persecute you" (Matthew 5:44).
  C. The critical question that we must ask ourselves: *Will we be extremists for love or extremists for hate?*

 II. Biblical love is active and goes beyond having pleasant feelings toward others.
  A. "God is love" and "whoever lives in love lives in God" (1 John 4:16).
  B. God's love *does* something. "Love is patient, love is kind . . . it always protects, always trusts, always hopes, always perseveres" (1 Corinthians 13:4, 7).
  C. Love must be the *foundation* of every effort that we have to heal and restore racial relationships.

 III. Love *unites.* It compels us to join with those who are different from us.
  A. The salvation Jesus came to offer was for all people (see Ephesians 2:14; Galatians 3:26–28).
  B. Tribalism divides humans into groups and builds walls. Unity tears down those walls.
  C. We need to seek out opportunities to be bridge builders.

 IV. Love is fully *present.* God broke through history to reach us.
  A. Love compels us to be present when those around us are treated unjustly.
  B. We build relationships with those who look, act, and think differently than us.
  C. We even step away from what is safe and practice loving our enemies.

 V. What do we do when we are facing hostility because of our faith?
  A. There is a two-step process we can follow in such situations:
   1. *Meditate* on the image of God in the person who is hostile to us.
   2. Verbally *praise* what you see in the other person that reflects the image of God.
  B. As we follow these steps, we are actively preventing their hostility from infecting our hearts.

NOTES

DISCUSS | 35 MINUTES

Now discuss what you just watched by answering the following questions.

1. Based on what you know of Dr. King and his work in the civil rights movement, would you describe him as an extremist for love? Why or why not? What are some of the characteristics you'd expect to find in an extremist for love?

2. How have you seen love in action in your life, church, or community? Would you refer to anyone in your community as an extremist for love? Explain.

3. How have you witnessed love show up for others and be present in your life, church, or community? How did you observe it impact others? Based on what you observed, do you agree that love should be the foundation to heal and restore racial divisions? Explain.

4. Do you see Sunday mornings as the most segregated time of the week? If you do see worship time as segregated, what might be done to make this time (or another hour in your week) less segregated? How might this help with restoring and healing racial divisions?

5. Have you ever felt as if you couldn't love your enemies—those people who are hostile to you? How could engaging in the two-step process of seeing the *image of God* in them and *verbally praising* what you see help in those situations?

RESPOND | 10 MINUTES

The following story from John 4:7–14 describes a time when Jesus "bridged the gap" and reached out to a person who had a different culture and background than his own. As you read, think of ways you can follow Jesus' example, and then answer the questions that follow.

> ⁷ When a Samaritan woman came to draw water, Jesus said to her, "Will you give me a drink?" ⁸ (His disciples had gone into the town to buy food.)
>
> ⁹ The Samaritan woman said to him, "You are a Jew and I am a Samaritan woman. How can you ask me for a drink?" (For Jews do not associate with Samaritans.)
>
> ¹⁰ Jesus answered her, "If you knew the gift of God and who it is that asks you for a drink, you would have asked him and he would have given you living water."
>
> ¹¹ "Sir," the woman said, "you have nothing to draw with and the well is deep. Where can you get this living water? ¹² Are you greater than our father Jacob, who gave us the well and drank from it himself, as did also his sons and his livestock?"
>
> ¹³ Jesus answered, "Everyone who drinks this water will be thirsty again, ¹⁴ but whoever drinks the water I give them will never thirst. Indeed, the water I give them will become in them a spring of water welling up to eternal life."

John notes that "Jews do not associate with Samaritans" (verse 9). What does this reveal about Jesus' intentions when he initiated a conversation with the woman?

John later writes that "many of the Samaritans from that town believed in [Jesus] because of the woman's testimony" (verse 39). What does this say about the impact of this conversation? What are some ways that you can "bridge the gap" with those who are different from you?

PRAY | 10 MINUTES

Praying for one another is one of the most important things you can do as a community. So make this time more than just a "closing prayer" to end your group experience by vulnerably sharing your prayers and how you are asking God to come through for you. Use the space below to write down any requests mentioned so you can pray for them in the week ahead.

Name   **Request**

_____ _____

_____ _____

_____ _____

_____ _____

_____ _____

_____ _____

_____ _____

_____ _____

_____ _____

_____ _____

PERSONAL STUDY

In this study, you are looking at some of the biblical principles that Dr. King embraced that enabled him to speak out and take action against the injustices he witnessed during the civil rights movement. In these weekly personal studies, you will take a deeper dive into exploring these principles, beginning with *love*, the focus of this session. The goal of these personal studies is to help you examine what the Bible has to say and how to apply those principles from God's Word to your life. As you work through each of these exercises, be sure to write down your responses to the questions, as you will be given a few minutes to share your insights at the start of the next session if you are doing this study with others.

STUDY 1

WHAT IS LOVE?

First Corinthians 13, known as the "love chapter," is a popular passage of Scripture that is often quoted at weddings and in sermons on love. But it can be surprising (and helpful) to review the descriptions of love in this chapter and ask yourself if you exhibit these same qualities. Those who consider themselves "extremists for love" like Jesus and Dr. King—or those who aspire to *be* extremists for love—should examine whether they exhibit the qualities of patience, kindness, humility, forgiveness, trust, hope, and perseverance that the apostle Paul describes.

When you put these descriptions of love into action in your life, you can better understand how Dr. King was able to truly forgive those who were hostile to him and even those who were violently threatening his life. You can see how the "drum major of justice" was able to keep pursuing what he felt was his God-given mission of unifying racial groups in spite of many attacks against him. Likewise, when you consider Jesus' actions—particularly how he was able to love those who were trying to destroy him—you can begin to understand what a powerful and transforming force love can be in our world today.

As you take steps toward unity and being fully present in relationships with those who are different from you, consider these models of Jesus, Dr. King, and Paul's words in 1 Corinthians 13 to evaluate your commitment to truly loving others. May we all become extremists for love as we pursue deeper relationships with God and our brothers and sisters.

> [4] Love is patient, love is kind. It does not envy, it does not boast, it is not proud. [5] It does not dishonor others, it is not self-seeking, it is not easily angered, it keeps no record of wrongs. [6] Love does not delight in evil but rejoices with the truth. [7] It always protects, always trusts, always hopes, always perseveres (1 Corinthians 13:4-7).

1. Write each description of love listed in this passage. Next to each word, write your own definition. If possible, think of an example of a time you either showed this kind of love or were shown it through the description. (For example, a time

when you showed love through being patient or a time when someone showed you love by being kind.)

2. Which words or phrases that describe love in this passage are particularly challenging to you in dealing with racial restoration? What other examples from Scripture can you use to help you meet the challenge of loving in this way for racial reconciliation?

3. What does it mean that "love does not delight in evil but rejoices with the truth" (verse 6)? In what ways have you rejected evil and stood up for truth as it relates to people who are different from you or who think differently than you do?

4. What does it mean that love "always protects, always trusts, always hopes, always perseveres" (verse 7)? What examples have you observed of people exemplifying these characteristics?

5. What does it mean that love "keeps no record of wrongs" (verse 5)? Why is this important in building bridges with those who are different from you? What can you do to actively release the record of wrongs people have done against you?

A Tender Heart

The gospel . . . demands a tender heart. Toughmindedness without tenderheartedness is cold and detached, leaving one's life in a perpetual winter devoid of the warmth of spring and the gentle heat of summer. What is more tragic than to see a person who has risen to the disciplined heights of toughmindedness but has at the same time sunk to the passionless depths of hardheartedness? . . .

Jesus frequently illustrated the characteristics of the hard-hearted. The rich fool was condemned, not because he was not toughminded, but rather because he was not tender-hearted. Life for him was a mirror in which he saw only himself, and not a window through which he saw other selves. [The rich man] went to hell, not because he was wealthy, but because he was not tenderhearted enough to see Lazarus and because he made no attempt to bridge the gulf between himself and his brother.

Jesus reminds us that the good life combines the tough-ness of the serpent and the tenderness of the dove. To have serpentlike qualities devoid of dovelike qualities is to be passionless, mean, and selfish. To have dovelike without serpentlike qualities is to be sentimental, anemic, and aimless. We must combine strongly marked antitheses. . . . A voice, echoing through the corridors of time, says to every intemperate Peter, "Put up thy sword." History is cluttered with the wreckage of nations that failed to follow Christ's command.

DR. MARTIN LUTHER KING JR.

FROM "THE STRENGTH TO LOVE," A COLLECTION OF SERMONS BY DR. KING PUBLISHED IN 1968[9]

STUDY 2

CALLED TO LOVE

As believers following Jesus' example to be extremists for love, we cannot hear enough the greatest love story of all. God's love for us—exemplified primarily through the gift and sacrifice of Jesus Christ—is the ultimate love story for humanity. It shows how, at just the right time, God met our biggest need (see Romans 5:6). He sent a Savior to rescue his people from the wages of sin and eternal death (see 6:23). Because of this selfless act of pure love, every man and woman who believes in Jesus is given eternal life.

In this study, we will review the love story of Jesus Christ to garner more fuel to commit to living as extremists for love. By reviewing and reflecting on the gift of grace that Jesus has provided to us, we can reinvigorate our mission to love one another as God has loved us. We can renew our commitment and stir up our passion to love fully regardless of our differences.

> 9 "As the Father has loved me, so have I loved you. Now remain in my love. 10 If you keep my commands, you will remain in my love, just as I have kept my Father's commands and remain in his love. 11 I have told you this so that my joy may be in you and that your joy may be complete. 12 My command is this: Love each other as I have loved you. 13 Greater love has no one than this: to lay down one's life for one's friends" (John 15:9–13).

1. Why is laying down one's life the greatest act of love that one can offer? Why do you think Jesus would mention laying down one's life for a friend in this passage? What does that say about how he might expect us to love each other?

2. First Peter 4:8 says, "love covers over a multitude of sins." How can love "cover" sin or wrongdoing? What challenges do you have with this? How can recalling

God's love for you through the sacrifice of Jesus help you show forgiveness when others wrong you?

---

⁷ Dear friends, let us love one another, for love comes from God. Everyone who loves has been born of God and knows God. ⁸ Whoever does not love does not know God, because God is love. ⁹ This is how God showed his love among us: He sent his one and only Son into the world that we might live through him. ¹⁰ This is love: not that we loved God, but that he loved us and sent his Son as an atoning sacrifice for our sins. ¹¹ Dear friends, since God so loved us, we also ought to love one another. . . .

¹⁹ We love because he first loved us. ²⁰ Whoever claims to love God yet hates a brother or sister is a liar. For whoever does not love their brother and sister, whom they have seen, cannot love God, whom they have not seen. ²¹ And he has given us this command: Anyone who loves God must also love their brother and sister (1 John 4:7–11,19–21).

---

3. What does John say is the source of all love (see verse 7)? How did God actively demonstrate the love that he had for each of us (see verse 9)?

4. What does John call the person who says he loves God but hates a brother or sister (see verse 20)? Why do you think this is so? How does Dr. King's message align with these words?

5. God is love, and God's love is active. Love is not a mere feeling; love does things. In light of injustice, discrimination, and abuse, love acts. How have you put love into action in the areas of discrimination, abuse, or injustice? How might you put love into action in these areas in the future?

LOVE YOUR ENEMIES

"Don't get your weapons. He who lives by the sword will perish by the sword. Remember that is what God said. We are not advocating violence. We want to love our enemies. Love them and let them know you love them."[10] These are the words King spoke to the angry crowd after his home was attacked in 1956. During this attack, his wife and children narrowly avoided death. The crowd was ready to seek revenge. Yet Dr. King's directive was to "love our enemies."

Jesus taught about loving one's enemies through example as well as in his parables. One such account is the parable of the unmerciful servant found in Matthew 18:23–34:

23 "Therefore, the kingdom of heaven is like a king who wanted to settle accounts with his servants. 24 As he began the settlement, a man who owed him ten thousand bags of gold was brought to him. 25 Since he was not able to pay, the master ordered that he and his wife and his children and all that he had be sold to repay the debt.

26 "At this the servant fell on his knees before him. 'Be patient with me,' he begged, 'and I will pay back everything.' 27 The servant's master took pity on him, canceled the debt and let him go.

28 "But when that servant went out, he found one of his fellow servants who owed him a hundred silver coins. He grabbed him and began to choke him. 'Pay back what you owe me!' he demanded.

29 "His fellow servant fell to his knees and begged him, 'Be patient with me, and I will pay it back.'

30 "But he refused. Instead, he went off and had the man thrown into prison until he could pay the debt. 31 When the other servants saw what had happened, they were outraged and went and told their master everything that had happened.

32 "Then the master called the servant in. 'You wicked servant,' he said, 'I canceled all that debt of yours because you begged me to. 33 Shouldn't you have had mercy on your fellow servant just as I had on you?' 34 In anger his master handed him over to the jailers to be tortured, until he should pay back all he owed.

The Power of Love

Now on the question of love or the love ethic, I think this is so important because hate is injurious to the hater as well as the hated. Many of the psychiatrists are telling us now that many of the strange things that happen in the subconscious and many of the inner conflicts are rooted in hate, and so they are now saying "love or perish." . . . It is necessary to follow the technique of nonviolence as the most potent weapon available to us, but it is necessary also to follow the love ethic which becomes a force of personality integration. . . .

I'm certainly not speaking of an affectionate response. I think it is really nonsense to urge oppressed peoples to love their oppressors in an affectionate sense. And I often call on the Greek language to aid me at this point because there are three words in the Greek for *love*. One is *eros*, which is sort of an aesthetic or a romantic love. Another is *philia*, which is sort of an intimate affection between personal friends; this is friendship, it is a reciprocal love and on this level, you love those people that you like. And then the Greek language comes out with the word *agape*, which is understanding, creative, redemptive good will for all men. . . .

And you come to the point of being able to love the person that does an evil deed in the sense of understanding and you can hate the deed that the person does. . . . I don't think of love, as in this context, as emotional bosh. I don't think of it as a weak force, but I think of love as something strong and that organizes itself into powerful direct action.

DR. MARTIN LUTHER KING JR.

FROM AN INTERVIEW WITH KENNETH B. CLARK
SOMETIME BEFORE AUGUST 28, 1963[11]

Jesus' words remind us of the cyclical relationship of forgiveness. Reading this parable as a story, we see it's about a king forgiving his servant, and then that same servant turning around and not forgiving someone else. But when read from the third-person—the outsider looking into this story—it should cause us to wonder about that unmerciful person: *How could he not let that go? He had just received mercy from the man he owed. He was released from a big debt—and he couldn't do the same for someone who owed him so much less?*

The challenge for us, the third-party observers, comes when Jesus explains the parable. Just as we expect the servant to return the favor and forgive the one who owes him a smaller debt than he's been forgiven, so God expects us to do the same. We have been forgiven of our sin through Christ's sacrifice—a cancellation of a great debt. Therefore, we are called to release others from the debts they owe us—because regardless of how painful they may be, they don't compare to the debt God has wiped out for us. We are called to be merciful servants. Even when it is tough and challenging, recalling the debt that has been canceled for us can push us to work toward forgiveness. It's a cycle we need to keep going.

1. Jesus begins his parable by stating that "the kingdom of heaven is like a king who wanted to settle accounts with his servants" (verse 23). What do you think Jesus was saying about how things operate in God's kingdom and for followers of Christ through this parable?

2. Jesus states in verse 35, "This is how my heavenly Father will treat each of you unless you forgive your brother or sister from your heart." How do these words from Jesus encourage you to work on forgiving those who have wronged you?

3. What role do you think forgiveness plays in racial reconciliation? Do you think forgiveness has a different role when it is personal versus when it is collective? Explain your response.

4. Jesus told this parable in response to a question from his disciple Peter: "Lord, how many times shall I forgive?" (verse 21). Peter wondered if forgiving the brother or sister who sinned against him "up to seven times" was enough. Jesus answered, "I tell you, not seven times, but seventy-seven times" (verse 22). Given the parable that followed, what do you think Jesus was trying to tell Peter? How does that message apply to us today?

5. What are some ways you can overcome the challenge to hold on to wrong-doings and not forgive your brother or sister? What does forgiveness look like to you even when you have to create boundaries for those who have repeatedly hurt you?

CONNECT & CATCH UP

Take time today to connect with a fellow group member and discuss the key insights from this session. Use any of the following prompts to help guide your discussion.

What are some ways that you want to mature in your relationship with God?

What is something you uncovered this week that made you feel convicted or that challenged you?

What do you want to work on in this study as it relates to showing more love through your actions?

What else do you hope to gain as you go through this study?

Use this time to go back and complete any of the study and reflection questions from previous days that you weren't able to finish. Make a note below of any revelations you've had and reflect on any growth or personal insights you've gained.

CONSCIENCE

If anyone, then, knows the good they ought to do and doesn't do it, it is sin for them.

JAMES 4:17

"This is no time to engage in the **luxury** of cooling off . . . now is the time to make **real** the **promises** of democracy."

Dr. Martin Luther King Jr.

WELCOME |

Dr. King not only preached about following one's conscience but also modeled the concept. On March 2, 1965, he issued his first public statement on the Vietnam War, denouncing it as "accomplishing nothing" and calling for peace. He followed this with an anti-war march in Chicago on March 25, 1967. At that march, he said, "The bombs in Vietnam explode at home—they destroy the dream and possibility for a decent America."[12]

Dr. King's stance was not embraced by everyone. His opposition to the war provoked criticism from Congress and strained his relations with President Lyndon B. Johnson. Yet Dr. King continued to speak out and act based on his conscience and what God, as revealed in his Word, was compelling him to do.

Following our conscience will not always be easy. It will often come with criticism and pushback from all sides. But when our conscience is rooted in the truth of God's Word, each of us—just like Dr. King—can find the strength and courage to stand up and act, regardless of the opposition. Our conscience will lead us to pursue the goals that are important to God's heart—truth, justice, and righteousness. It will also enable us to fulfill the commission that Jesus gave to us to love our neighbor as we love ourselves (see Mark 12:31).

When we think of *loving* ourselves, we do not think of *harming* ourselves. Likewise, when we think of loving our neighbors as ourselves, we understand that implies a certain way of treating others. We do not keep silent when we see an injustice, because that is actually betraying our neighbor and not standing up for the values that are important to God. Instead, our conscience compels us to speak out—and, more importantly, take action—for the good of all, knowing that our silence and our inaction will indeed be too costly.

CONNECT | 15 MINUTES

Get the session started by choosing one of these questions to discuss as a group:

- What is something that spoke to your heart in last week's personal study that you would like to share with the group?

  — or —

- What does it look like to follow your conscience? Share an example of a time you followed your conscience in a manner that went against cultural norms.

WATCH | 20 MINUTES

Now watch the video for this session. Below is an outline of the key points covered during the teaching. Record any thoughts or concepts that stand out to you.

OUTLINE

I. Many experts agree that our society is more divided today than at any time since the Civil War.
   A. Christians are the body of Christ established to bring healing to a broken world.
   B. Now is the time to learn from the wisdom of those who have walked before us.
   C. Now is the time to invite the Spirit of God to reshape our broken reality.
II. Conscience is the inner witness of our hearts about what is right or wrong.
   A. Conscience plays a key role in helping us do what is right.
   B. A weak conscience yields to cultural norms of prejudice, selfishness, or segregation.
   C. A strong conscience puts into action Jesus' command to love our neighbors as ourselves.
III. Jesus gives us a new and clean conscience.
   A. A pure conscience will help us stand for what is right in the face of racism.
   B. We can listen to our consciences and bridge the canyon of hate.
   C. We can follow in the footsteps of those who over centuries have done just that.
IV. Following our conscience means always doing the right thing before God.
   A. Dr. King's peaceful breaking of the law to follow his conscience is called *civil disobedience.*
   B. Dr. King made a crucial distinction between civil disobedience and anarchy.
   C. Following our conscience means not following laws that are in conflict with God's principles.
V. We have to be willing to pay the price for doing what we know is right.
   A. As people of conscience, we must ask, "What causes do we believe in enough to act on?"
   B. Remaining silent when we see an injustice is betraying our conscience.
   C. Our conscience must guide us to make choices to love as Jesus taught us to love.

NOTES

DISCUSS | 35 MINUTES

Discuss what you just watched by answering the following questions.

1. Many experts say that our society is more divided today than at any time since the Civil War. Do you agree with this assertion? Explain your response.

2. God instructed his people, "Learn to do right; seek justice. Defend the oppressed. Take up the cause of the fatherless; plead the case of the widow" (Isaiah 1:17). Do you agree or disagree with the statement made in the teaching that the body of Christ has been on the "sidelines" when it comes to issues of discrimination and justice? Explain your response.

3. How should our conscience play a role in helping us to do what God says is right? Why is it important to have this conscience shaped by the truths in God's Word?

4. The apostle Paul wrote, "So from now on we regard no one from a worldly point of view. Though we once regarded Christ in this way, we do so no longer. Therefore, if anyone is in Christ, the new creation has come: The old has gone, the new is here! All this is from God, who reconciled us to himself through Christ and gave us the ministry of reconciliation" (2 Corinthians 5:16–18). How can believing in Jesus give us a new, clean conscience?

5. What distinction did Dr. King make between civil disobedience and anarchy? Why is this a critical distinction for those engaging in the ministry of justice?

RESPOND | 10 MINUTES

Paul often faced negative attacks against his character and had to defend his actions and motives. The following passage from 2 Corinthians 1:12–14 is one such instance in which he had to respond to his accusers. Read what Paul says about his conscience being clean and his defense of the way he conducted himself, and then answer the questions that follow.

> [12] Now this is our boast: Our conscience testifies that we have conducted ourselves in the world, and especially in our relations with you, with integrity and godly sincerity. We have done so, relying not on worldly wisdom but on God's grace. [13] For we do not write you anything you cannot read or understand. And I hope that, [14] as you have understood us in part, you will come to understand fully that you can boast of us just as we will boast of you in the day of the Lord Jesus.

How did Paul say that he and the other apostles acted toward those with whom they shared the gospel? What does Paul say that their conscience "testified" about them?

What does your conscience "testify" about your words and actions? How much do you rely on your conscience to make decisions? Explain.

PRAY | 10 MINUTES

End your time by praying as a group. Ask God to continue to give you the courage to speak and act as you follow your conscience and share the dream with others. Use the space below to write down any requests mentioned so you can pray for them in the week ahead.

Name	Request

PERSONAL STUDY

In the first personal study, you looked at *love* as the foundation of the Christian message as well as the foundation to restoring relationships. As you explored God's extreme love for you, made evident through the gift of eternal life provided in Christ, you highlighted some specific features and actions of love. In this personal study, you will look at the principle of *conscience* and how it convicts you and pushes you to stand up for what is right. Prayerfully reflect on the questions as you stretch yourself for the challenging work to repair and reshape our broken world.

WHAT IS CONSCIENCE?

Because we are humans, we do not always follow our God-given conscience when it points us to doing good. Silence, apathy, and excuses are all results of us not following our conscience. We talk ourselves into not acting when we are fearful, or decide our voice doesn't matter, or give in to indecision because we are not clear on how we're called to be our brothers' and sisters' keeper. It is only when we acknowledge we have a conscience to help us make the right choice that we step toward operating in love.

Using the Word of God, as well as God's Spirit of truth, to direct our minds and our decisions is one way to proof-test our conscience. As Paul writes, "All Scripture is God-breathed and is useful for teaching, rebuking, correcting and training in righteousness" (2 Timothy 3:16). If our decisions align with the truth of God's Word, it means we are on the right track. But if those decisions stray from God's Word—and the Spirit of God—we know we are in trouble.

How will we know when we have strayed? Most of us will feel *convicted* in some way . . . a recognition of how our sin has dishonored God (see Psalm 5:4) and an unsettled feeling that will remain until we take steps to resolve it. An unsettled mind is always the opposite of the peace that God gives to those who seek him—a peace that Paul says "transcends all understanding" and guards our hearts and our minds in Christ Jesus (Philippians 4:7).

> ¹³ The blood of goats and bulls and the ashes of a heifer sprinkled on those who are ceremonially unclean sanctify them so that they are outwardly clean. ¹⁴ How much more, then, will the blood of Christ, who through the eternal Spirit offered himself unblemished to God, cleanse our consciences from acts that lead to death, so that we may serve the living God! (Hebrews 9:13–14).

1. In this passage, the author compares what happened when we were cleansed by animals' blood under the Old Testament sacrificial systems and what happens now under the New Testament system when we are cleansed by Jesus'

blood. What is the difference between the cleansings? Which one cleanses our conscience? Why do you think this is the case?

> [12] Jesus entered the temple courts and drove out all who were buying and selling there. He overturned the tables of the money changers and the benches of those selling doves. [13] "It is written," he said to them, "'My house will be called a house of prayer,' but you are making it 'a den of robbers'" (Matthew 21:12–13).

2. Jesus saw that the temple was being misused. What had been intended to be a house of worship was being used as a venue for commerce. Even worse, the money changers were working alongside the merchants to make a profit, and their priorities had nothing to do with God. How did Jesus seek to address this injustice that was taking place? What does this say to you about following your conscience and taking action when you see an injustice?

> [10] On a Sabbath Jesus was teaching in one of the synagogues, [11] and a woman was there who had been crippled by a spirit for eighteen years. . . . [13] Then [Jesus] put his hands on her, and immediately she straightened up and praised God. [14] Indignant because Jesus had healed on the Sabbath, the synagogue leader said to the people, "There are six days for work. So come and be healed on those days, not on the Sabbath." [15] The Lord answered him, "You hypocrites! Doesn't each of you on the Sabbath untie your ox or donkey from the stall and lead it out to give it water? [16] Then should not this woman, a daughter of Abraham, whom Satan has kept bound for eighteen long years, be set free on the Sabbath day from what bound her?" (Luke 13:10–11, 13–16).

Obliged by Conscience

It is many months now since I found myself obliged by conscience to end my silence and to take a public stand against my country's war in Vietnam. The considerations which led me to that painful decision have not disappeared; indeed, they have been magnified by the course of events since then. The war itself is intensified; the impact on my country is even more destructive. I cannot speak about the great themes of violence and nonviolence, of social change and of hope for the future, without reflecting on the tremendous violence of Vietnam.

Since the spring of 1967, when I first made public my opposition to my government's policy, many persons have questioned me about the wisdom of my decision. "Why *you*?" they have said. "Peace and civil rights don't mix. Aren't you hurting the cause of your people?" And when I hear such questions, I have been greatly saddened, for they mean that the inquirers have never really known me, my commitment, or my calling. . . .

Somehow this madness must cease. We must stop now. I speak as a child of God and brother to the suffering poor of Vietnam. I speak for those whose land is being laid waste, whose homes are being destroyed, whose culture is being subverted. I speak for the poor of America who are paying the double price of smashed hopes at home and death and corruption in Vietnam. I speak as a citizen of the world, for the world as it stands is aghast at the path we have taken. . . . The great initiative in this war is ours. The initiative to stop it must be ours.

Dr. Martin Luther King Jr.

FROM "CONSCIENCE AND THE VIETNAM WAR," SERMON
AIRED BY THE CANADIAN BROADCASTING CORPORATION
FROM NOVEMBER–DECEMBER 1967[13]

3. Why did the synagogue leader become "indignant" when he saw Jesus heal the woman? How did Jesus reply to him? What issue was Jesus calling out when he spoke to the leader?

[9] [Jesus] continued, "You have a fine way of setting aside the commands of God in order to observe your own traditions! [10] For Moses said, 'Honor your father and mother,' and, 'Anyone who curses their father or mother is to be put to death.' [11] But you say that if anyone declares that what might have been used to help their father or mother is Corban (that is, devoted to God)— [12] then you no longer let them do anything for their father or mother. [13] Thus you nullify the word of God by your tradition that you have handed down. And you do many things like that" (Mark 7:9–13).

4. Jesus spoke these words to "the Pharisees and some of the teachers of the law" (verse 1). How were these religious leader canceling, or nullifying, the Word of God that had been passed down to them? What were they using to cancel God's Word?

5. How can you avoid this same kind of action, or inaction, in your relationship with other people? What do Jesus' words say to you as it relates to following your good conscience?

FOLLOW YOUR CONSCIENCE

The great English preacher Charles Spurgeon is attributed as saying, "A Bible that is falling apart usually belongs to someone who isn't." His statement alludes to the truth that studying the Bible—often to the point that its pages are folded and separating from the seams—leads to a life that is full and a person who is able to weather any storms. Now, today this may or may not be the case—more and more people have different Bibles as well as apps and other means to accessing God's Word—but there is some plausibility in the underlying concept.

This is especially true when we consider how our conscience can be informed by the *truth* of God's Word. The Bible tells us that God, at his core, is loving (see 1 John 4:8) and describes many aspects of his nature (see, for example, Numbers 14:18; Deuteronomy 32:4; Zephaniah 3:17). By studying Scripture, we grow to know God better, which can develop trust and faith in him and produce a conscience that is aligned with his good and perfect will.

Understanding what God stands for and expects of us then leads us to growth and the ability to act in righteousness. The more we know about God, the more we trust him and the more our conscience becomes aligned with his truth. We develop an inner compass that points toward God and what he would have us to do. Immersing ourselves within the Word builds within us a God-centered and truth-filled conscience—one we can follow throughout our lives.

[10] Finally, be strong in the Lord and in his mighty power. [11] Put on the full armor of God, so that you can take your stand against the devil's schemes. [12] For our struggle is not against flesh and blood, but against the rulers, against the authorities, against the powers of this dark world and against the spiritual forces of evil in the heavenly realms. [13] Therefore put on the full armor of God, so that when the day of evil comes, you may be able to stand your ground, and after you have done everything, to stand. [14] Stand firm then, with the belt of truth

buckled around your waist, with the breastplate of righteousness in place, [15] and with your feet fitted with the readiness that comes from the gospel of peace. [16] In addition to all this, take up the shield of faith, with which you can extinguish all the flaming arrows of the evil one. [17] Take the helmet of salvation and the sword of the Spirit, which is the word of God (Ephesians 6:10–17).

1. Paul uses the imagery of a Roman soldier in this passage to demonstrate how we should "put on" the armor of God every day. Who does Paul say that we are fighting or struggling against? How can recognizing who our true enemy is help us to stand up for God's righteousness?

2. We are to put on the full armor of God so that we are prepared "when the day of evil comes" (verse 13). This "day of evil" could include temptations that come your way. How does knowing and following God's Word enable you to stand your ground against these kinds of attacks? How does it strengthen your conscience to do what is right?

3. Notice the various pieces of armor—the belt of truth, breastplate of righteousness, shoes of the gospel of peace, shield of faith, helmet of salvation, and sword of the Spirit. What does it look like for you to "put on" each of these different pieces of armor?

The Urgency of Now

We are confronted with the fierce urgency of now. In this unfolding conundrum of life and history there is such a thing as being too late. Procrastination is still the thief of time. Life often leaves us standing here, naked and dejected with a lost opportunity. The "tide in the affairs of men" does not remain at the flood; it ebbs. We may cry out desperately for time to pause in her passage, but time is deaf to every plea and rushes on. Over the bleached bones and jumbled residue of numerous civilizations are written the pathetic words: "Too late." There is an invisible book of life that faithfully records our vigilance or our neglect. . . .

We must move past indecision to action. . . . If we do not act we shall surely be dragged down the long dark and shameful corridors of time reserved for those who possess power without compassion, might without morality, and strength without sight.

Now let us begin. Now let us rededicate ourselves to the long and bitter—but beautiful—struggle for a new world. This is the calling of the sons of God, and our brothers wait eagerly for our response. Shall we say the odds are too great? Shall we tell them the struggle is too hard? Will our message be that the forces of American life militate against their arrival as full men, and we send our deepest regrets? Or will there be another message, or longing, of hope, of solidarity with their yearnings, of commitment to their cause, whatever the cost?

DR. MARTIN LUTHER KING JR.

FROM "A TIME TO BREAK SILENCE," SPEECH DELIVERED AT THE RIVERSIDE CHURCH IN NEW YORK CITY ON APRIL 4, 1967[14]

4. Which piece of armor do you need to pay more attention to putting on every day? What would you need to do or change to be better equipped with that piece of armor?

[18] And pray in the Spirit on all occasions with all kinds of prayers and requests. With this in mind, be alert and always keep on praying for all the Lord's people. [19] Pray also for me, that whenever I speak, words may be given me so that I will fearlessly make known the mystery of the gospel, [20] for which I am an ambassador in chains. Pray that I may declare it fearlessly, as I should (Ephesians 6:18–20).

5. What role does prayer have in fighting against evil and standing strong in the Lord? How does this apply to having a God-centered conscience?

DO THE RIGHT THING

Those who follow their God-given conscience are also people of integrity. They do what is right even when no one is looking. In fact, they do what is right *especially* when no one is looking. Taking a stand for righteousness will always require integrity on our part.

When we are not directly impacted by an injustice, it can be easy for us to remain silent about the offense or even ignore that it is happening. We say nothing when an offensive word or joke is spoken. We do nothing about policies we know will harm those whom Jesus told us to look after and love. We stay in our segregated coves, surrounding ourselves with those who look like us, act like us, and live like us. No one questions those who do not make waves, so we can quickly get lulled into just keeping the status quo and not taking action.

However, a God-centered conscience will not allow us to rest when we see an injustice. Our call to bring about God's kingdom on earth will ring, alerting us to the fact that what we are witnessing is not in God's will and demands us to speak up and take action. "Do the right thing" is more than a catchphrase. It's a cry from inside that compels us to live with integrity and act even when we could stay silent—or perhaps *especially* when we could remain silent. If we have integrity, we will do what is right when no one is looking. We will choose to do what is right because our conscience is guiding us and won't let us rest until we stand up and speak out.

> [6] Among those who were chosen were some from Judah: Daniel, Hananiah, Mishael and Azariah. [7] The chief official gave them new names: to Daniel, the name Belteshazzar; to Hananiah, Shadrach; to Mishael, Meshach; and to Azariah, Abednego. [8] But Daniel resolved not to defile himself with the royal food and wine, and he asked the chief official for permission not to defile himself this way (Daniel 1:6–8).

1. Daniel and his three friends (among others) had been taken from Jerusalem by King Nebuchadnezzar's armies and were now being trained to serve the king in Babylon. As part of their training, they were given the best food and drink. But this presented a problem for Daniel and his friends, as some of the food and drink was either forbidden to them under Jewish law or had been offered to pagan gods. What action did Daniel and the others take to address this problem? How does this reveal they had God-given integrity?

> [1] King Nebuchadnezzar made an image of gold, sixty cubits high and six cubits wide, and set it up on the plain of Dura in the province of Babylon. . . . [4] Then the herald loudly proclaimed, "Nations and peoples of every language, this is what you are commanded to do: [5] As soon as you hear the sound of the horn, flute, zither, lyre, harp, pipe and all kinds of music, you must fall down and worship the image of gold that King Nebuchadnezzar has set up. [6] Whoever does not fall down and worship will immediately be thrown into a blazing furnace" (Daniel 3:1, 4–6).

2. This story occurs sometime after Daniel and his friends arrived in Babylon for their training. What did the king command all of his subjects to do when they heard the sound of the music? What was the penalty for anyone who did not follow the king's decree?

> [16] Shadrach, Meshach and Abednego replied to him, "King Nebuchadnezzar, we do not need to defend ourselves before you in this matter. [17] If we are thrown into the blazing furnace, the God we serve is able to deliver us from it,

and he will deliver us from Your Majesty's hand. [18] But even if he does not, we want you to know, Your Majesty, that we will not serve your gods or worship the image of gold you have set up" (Daniel 3:16–18).

3. What reasons did Shadrach, Meshach, and Abednego give for not following the law? What does this response say about their integrity and dedication to God?

4. Shadrach, Meshach, and Abednego proclaimed that God *was able* to deliver them from the fiery furnace but that *even if he did not,* they would still not serve the king's gods. What were they acknowledging about God's ways (see Isaiah 55:8–9)? What does this portion of their response reveal about their convictions and faith in a sovereign God?

5. Dr. Martin Luther King Jr. taught that moral disobedience occurs when we follow our consciences with respect to unjust human laws that are in clear conflict with God's principles. How do these stories describe civil disobedience as Dr. King described it?

CONNECT & CATCH UP

Take time today to connect with a fellow group member and discuss the key insights from this session. Use any of the following prompts to help guide your discussion.

What ideas stood out to you as it relates to following your conscience?

What does it look like in practical terms to make your conscience "captive" to the Word of God?

How does the Word of God help your conscience to stay pure so you can live with integrity?

What is the difference between civil disobedience and anarchy?

Use this time to go back and complete any of the study and reflection questions from previous days that you weren't able to finish. Make a note below of any revelations you've had and reflect on any growth or personal insights you've gained.

COLORED
WAITING ROOM

JUSTICE

*Righteousness and justice are the
foundation of your throne;
love and faithfulness go before you.*

PSALM 89:14

"Now is the time to make **justice a reality** for all of God's children."

Dr. Martin Luther King Jr.

WELCOME |

On September 18, 1963, a grieving crowd gathered to hear Dr. King deliver a eulogy in Birmingham, Alabama. Two days before, on a quiet Sunday morning, a dynamite bomb had exploded in the back stairwell of the Sixteenth Street Baptist Church, killing four African American girls and wounding more than twenty others. In his seven-minute address, Dr. King chose to comfort the crowd as well as challenge them with his words.[15]

Instead of retaliation, Dr. King called for hope, understanding, forgiveness, and respect. He said, "We must not become bitter; nor must we harbor the desire to retaliate with violence. . . . Somehow we must believe that the most misguided among them can learn to respect the dignity and worth of all human personality."[16] On that day, Dr. King spoke of a justice that restores people and views even the brutal offender as a part of humanity.

Restorative justice accomplishes this through the restoration of a relationship where the wrong is fixed through merciful means. Restorative justice considers the humanity of the offenders and views them as more than just their offense—it sees them as children of God rather than as the totality of their actions. Jesus' work on the cross is the ultimate example of this kind of justice. Through his death and resurrection, he paid the price that God's justice demanded as a penalty for our sin. His actions on the cross enabled a broken and fallen humanity to once again enter into relationship with a holy God.

Just imagine what our world would be like if we practiced this kind of justice. A kind of justice where we were quick to renew and restore . . . where we viewed an offense as an opportunity to mend a relationship . . . where we refused to label a person by his or her wrongful actions. Restorative justice allows righteousness and justice to operate in tandem and reflects the very throne of God, where truth, love, and mercy reside.

CONNECT | 15 MINUTES

Get the session started by choosing one of these questions to discuss as a group:

- What is something that spoke to your heart in last week's personal study that you would like to share with the group?

  — or —

- What do you think is the difference between justice and mercy? Explain.

WATCH | 20 MINUTES

Now watch the video for this session. Below is an outline of the key points covered during the teaching. Record any thoughts or concepts that stand out to you.

OUTLINE

I. Dr. King delivered a eulogy for four girls killed in a bombing in Birmingham.
   A. Dr. King encouraged the mourners not to become bitter or retaliate with violence.
   B. Genesis 1 reminds us that God made everyone in his image—the *imago dei*.
   C. Every human is inherently valuable, which is the foundation to justice.
II. Righteousness and justice are often paired throughout Scripture.
   A. Righteousness means a "right-ness," particularly in relationships.
   B. Justice "makes right" a relationship in which a human being is treated as less valuable than another.
III. There are two main categories for justice.
   A. *Retributive justice* is about making a situation right by having the guilty party suffer punishment.
   B. *Restorative justice* is about helping people return to the place of worth that God intended.
   C. God is concerned about restorative justice (see Leviticus 25).
IV. The life and teaching of Jesus is the most compelling example of restorative and retributive justice.
   A. Jesus described a day of judgment for everyone to give an account of their actions and receive either eternal blessing or eternal punishment (retributive justice).
   B. Jesus' mission, quoted in Luke 4:18–19, describes his plans to bring freedom to prisoners and the oppressed and restore sight to the blind (restorative justice).
   C. Jesus' example reveals that when injustice exists, we should look for a creative solution that makes right the damage done for both the oppressed and the oppressor.
V. To be people of restorative justice means to make others' problems our own.
   A. We ask questions to find out who is suffering and who God is calling us to help.
   B. We serve as a conduit of God's love by standing up for those who have been wronged.

NOTES

_____

_____

_____

_____

_____

_____

_____

_____

_____

_____

_____

_____

_____

_____

DISCUSS | 35 MINUTES

Discuss what you just watched by answering the following questions.

1. *Retributive* justice is about making a situation right by having the guilty party suffer punishment, while *restorative* justice is about helping the guilty return to the place of worth that God intended for them. When have you witnessed each of these types of justice?

2. In Dr. King's eulogy for the four girls killed in the bombing of the Sixteenth Street Baptist Church, he told the grieving crowd, "We must not become bitter, nor must we harbor the desire to retaliate with violence . . . we must believe that the most misguided among them can learn to respect the dignity and worth of all human personality." How does this represent a call for restorative justice?

3. Paul wrote that in the body of Christ, "There is neither Jew nor Gentile, neither slave nor free . . . for you are all one in Christ Jesus" (Galatians 3:28). What are some examples you have seen of people *not* being treated as equal before God because of their race or other trait? What could you do to model restorative justice in those situations?

4. The Jews in first-century Israel were expecting the Messiah to bring retributive justice and overthrow their Roman rulers. How did Jesus broaden their definition of justice by also teaching and modeling restorative justice? What was his ultimate act of restorative justice?

5. What is your obligation when people around you have been hurt? What are some of the challenges in thinking of creative solutions to a problem that the harm has created?

RESPOND | 10 MINUTES

Jesus' death on the cross satisfied the penalty for sin under retributive justice but was also an act of restorative justice in that it brought us back into relationship with God. Read what Paul says about Christ's sacrifice in Romans 5:6–11, and then answer the questions that follow.

> [6] You see, at just the right time, when we were still powerless, Christ died for the ungodly. [7] Very rarely will anyone die for a righteous person, though for a good person someone might possibly dare to die. [8] But God demonstrates his own love for us in this: While we were still sinners, Christ died for us. [9] Since we have now been justified by his blood, how much more shall we be saved from God's wrath through him! [10] For if, while we were God's enemies, we were reconciled to him through the death of his Son, how much more, having been reconciled, shall we be saved through his life! [11] Not only is this so, but we also boast in God through our Lord Jesus Christ, through whom we have now received reconciliation.

What does Paul say that Jesus did for us at "just the right time"? How does Jesus' death on the cross represent God's ultimate act of love toward us?

Paul says we can rejoice because we have received reconciliation with a holy God. What does this say about the role we are called to play in reconciliation with others?

PRAY | 10 MINUTES

Seeking God in prayer can be especially helpful when you are working toward re-storative justice. So use this time to ask God to speak to you about your role in bringing about restoration in relationships where there has been harm. Close your time by using the space below to write down any requests so you can continue to pray about them in the week ahead.

Name   **Request**

PERSONAL STUDY

In the previous personal study, you looked at the principle of *conscience* and how it convicts and compels you to stand up for what is right. You explored how conscience is the inner witness of your heart about what is right and wrong in light of God's truth and righteousness. In this personal study, you will look more closely at the principle of retributive and restorative justice as modeled by Christ. Use these studies to think about the challenges of each category of justice and the role you play in reminding all of God's people that we are made in his image.

STUDY 1

WHAT IS JUSTICE?

Depending on where we stand in a given situation, our view of justice may change. When we are harmed or are the victim, we want God to come swiftly, exact vengeance on the perpetrators, and set things straight. We may even desire to take the reins and seek revenge ourselves. We have some ideas of how the perpetrators can be punished!

But the tables turn when we are the ones in the wrong and mistreat others . . . whether that is intentionally, through policies, or even through silence. In those instances, we want the grace and mercy of God to fall on us. Yet it is more important to consider how our views of righteousness and justice align with *God's* views as seen through the pages of his Word. How do our views look different when we think of God in justice and righteousness?

In the Bible, we see righteousness and justice working together. We find justice in the form of retribution *and* restoration, where the goal is for us to be restored to our humanity before God, where all people are seen as the *imago dei*—the image of God. Remembering the humanity of a person, and their connection to the Creator, shifts our focus when seeking righteousness and justice. We begin to seek restoration even when retribution is required, knowing that how we seek justice impacts our unity and reconciliation as people of God.

These children—unoffending, innocent and beautiful—were the victims of one of the most vicious, heinous crimes ever perpetrated against humanity. Yet they died nobly . . . [and] have something to say to us in their death. . . . They say to each of us, black and white alike, that we must substitute courage for caution. They say to us that we must be concerned not merely about who murdered them, but about the system, the way of life, the philosophy which produced the murderers. Their death says to us that we must work passionately and unrelentingly for the realization of the American dream.[17]

1. Dr. King gave these remarks at the eulogy for the four little girls who were killed in the bombing in Birmingham. How did Dr. King say to the mourners that they should respond to this injustice? How are his words an example of restorative justice?

> [30] "A man was going down from Jerusalem to Jericho, when he was attacked by robbers. They stripped him of his clothes, beat him and went away, leaving him half dead. [31] A priest happened to be going down the same road, and when he saw the man, he passed by on the other side. [32] So too, a Levite, when he came to the place and saw him, passed by on the other side. [33] But a Samaritan, as he traveled, came where the man was; and when he saw him, he took pity on him. [34] He went to him and bandaged his wounds, pouring on oil and wine. Then he put the man on his own donkey, brought him to an inn and took care of him. [35] The next day he took out two denarii and gave them to the innkeeper. 'Look after him,' he said, 'and when I return, I will reimburse you for any extra expense you may have'" (Luke 10:30-35).

2. In this week's group time, you looked at three assumptions that underlie restorative justice: (1) when people and relationships are harmed, needs are created; (2) the needs created by the harms lead to obligation; and (3) the obligation is to heal and "put right" the harms. Look at these underlying assumptions in the parable told by Christ. What was the injustice done? What was the need created by the injustice? What was the creative solution?

3. A person of restorative justice will go beyond merely asking *who has been hurt*, *what are the needs*, and *who has the obligation to address the needs.* Rather, a person of restorative justice will become the method of "putting right" the harm done to others. How did the Good Samaritan in Jesus' parable reveal that he was a person of restorative justice?

A Philosophy of Life

We have come to the point where there is no longer a choice now between nonviolence and riots. It must be militant, massive nonviolence, or riots. The discontent is so deep, the anger so ingrained, the despair, the restlessness so wide, that something has to be brought into being to serve as a channel through which these deep emotional feelings, these deep angry feelings, can be funneled. There has to be an outlet . . .

I'm committed to nonviolence absolutely. I'm just not going to kill anybody, whether it's in Vietnam or here. I'm not going to burn down any building. If nonviolent protest fails this summer, I will continue to preach it and teach it, and we at the Southern Christian Leadership Conference will still do this. I plan to stand by nonviolence because I have found it to be a philosophy of life that regulates not only my dealings in the struggle for racial justice but also my dealings with people, with my own self. I will still be faithful to nonviolence.

But I'm frank enough to admit that if our nonviolent campaign doesn't generate some progress, people are just going to engage in more violent activity. . . . In any event, we will not have been the ones who will have failed. We will place the problems of the poor at the seat of government of the wealthiest nation in the history of mankind. If that power refuses to acknowledge its debt to the poor, it will have failed to live up to its promise to insure "life, liberty and the pursuit of happiness" to its citizens.

DR. MARTIN LUTHER KING JR.

FROM THE ARTICLE "SHOWDOWN FOR NONVIOLENCE," PUBLISHED IN *LOOK* MAGAZINE ON APRIL 16, 1968[18]

> ³ The teachers of the law and the Pharisees brought in a woman caught in adultery. They made her stand before the group ⁴ and said to Jesus, "Teacher, this woman was caught in the act of adultery. ⁵ In the Law Moses commanded us to stone such women. Now what do you say?" ⁶ They were using this question as a trap, in order to have a basis for accusing him. But Jesus bent down and started to write on the ground with his finger. ⁷ When they kept on questioning him, he straightened up and said to them, "Let any one of you who is without sin be the first to throw a stone at her." ⁸ Again he stooped down and wrote on the ground. ⁹ At this, those who heard began to go away one at a time, the older ones first, until only Jesus was left, with the woman still standing there. ¹⁰ Jesus straightened up and asked her, "Woman, where are they? Has no one condemned you?" ¹¹ "No one, sir," she said. "Then neither do I condemn you," Jesus declared. "Go now and leave your life of sin" (John 8:3–11).

4. In this story, who was harmed? What need was created from this harm? Whose obligation was it to create the solution? Who actually participated in restorative justice?

5. Think about the concerns you have when it comes to extending restorative justice. Do you think it would be possible to extend this type of justice to others who have *harmed* you? Why or why not? What would be the benefits if you were able to do this for others?

BEYOND YOURSELF

At the crux of restorative justice—where we seek to make perpetrators and victims whole—is *humility* and *selflessness*. Restorative justice looks out for our neighbors and even takes on their problems as our own. When someone—or some group in society—is harmed, we are quick to spot the need. We don't just look at what has happened and say, *"It isn't my business,"* or *"It doesn't impact my community,"* or *"I just can't get involved."* No, a justice seeker sees the need and acts to restore the parties involved to their true level of humanity . . . the *imago dei*.

Now, an honest survey of what it takes to be a justice seeker produces challenges for us. It is not an easy role for us to accept, because it is not a natural position for us to deny ourselves and consider others above ourselves. It requires humility, courage, and an attitude that models Christ, who, "being in very nature God, did not consider equality with God something to be used to his own advantage" (Philippians 2:6).

Do you have the heart of a justice seeker? Can you look beyond yourself and answer the call of those who have been harmed? Do you consider yourself your brothers' and sisters' keeper even when what is harmful seems to be in another community or in another neighborhood? Do you desire for God to give you a heart to live selflessly and restore justice in our world?

> [5] Have the same mindset as Christ Jesus: [6] who, being in very nature God, did not consider equality with God something to be used to his own advantage; [7] rather, he made himself nothing by taking the very nature of a servant, being made in human likeness. [8] And being found in appearance as a man, he humbled himself by becoming obedient to death—even death on a cross! (Philippians 2:5–8).

1. How did Jesus demonstrate humility? How are we to follow his example in our relationships? How does this relate to our role in restorative justice?

⁵ May the God who gives endurance and encouragement give you the same attitude of mind toward each other that Christ Jesus had, ⁶ so that with one mind and one voice you may glorify the God and Father of our Lord Jesus Christ. ⁷ Accept one another, then, just as Christ accepted you, in order to bring praise to God (Romans 15:5–7).

2. What "attitude of mind" did Jesus have toward us? How can adopting the "same attitude of mind toward each other that Christ Jesus had" help you work toward restorative justice?

¹ As a prisoner for the Lord, then, I urge you to live a life worthy of the calling you have received. ² Be completely humble and gentle; be patient, bearing with one another in love. ³ Make every effort to keep the unity of the Spirit through the bond of peace. ⁴ There is one body and one Spirit, just as you were called to one hope when you were called; ⁵ one Lord, one faith, one baptism; ⁶ one God and Father of all, who is over all and through all and in all (Ephesians 4:1–6).

3. "Live a life worthy of the calling you have received" (verse 1). What is the "calling" that followers of Jesus have received? How does this calling relate to unity? What role do you play in bringing about unity in the body of Christ?

Just vs. Unjust Laws

There are two types of laws. There are just laws and there are unjust laws. . . . Men and women have a moral obligation to obey just and right laws . . . [and] we must see that there are unjust laws. Now the question comes into being, what is the difference, and who determines the difference, between a just and unjust law?

A just law is a law that squares with a moral law. It is a law that squares with that which is right, so that any law that uplifts human personality is a just law. Whereas that law which is out of harmony with the moral is a law which does not square with the moral law of the universe. It does not square with the law of God, so for that reason it is unjust, and any law that degrades the human personality is an unjust law. . . . I would go on to say in more concrete terms than an unjust law is a code that the majority inflicts on the minority that is not binding on itself. So that this becomes difference made legal. . . .

Now the same token of a just law would be just the opposite. A just law becomes saneness made legal. It is a code that the majority, who happen to believe in that code, compel the minority, who don't believe in it, to follow, because they are willing to follow it themselves, so it is saneness made legal. Therefore the individuals who stand up on the basis of civil disobedience realize that they are following something that says that there are just laws and there are unjust laws.

DR. MARTIN LUTHER KING JR.

FROM AN ADDRESS BEFORE THE ANNUAL MEETING OF THE FELLOWSHIP OF THE CONCERNED ON NOVEMBER 16, 1961[19]

4. The term *imago dei* suggests that humans have the same "likeness" as God—the ability to have the same moral attributes as God. We can love, we can be good, we can be selfless, and the like. Think of some attributes of God that you have observed in others. What are they? How can recognizing these God-given attributes help you to treat others justly?

He has shown you, O mortal, what is good.
    And what does the LORD require of you?
To act justly and to love mercy
    and to walk humbly with your God (Micah 6:8).

5. What does it mean to "act justly," "love mercy," and "walk humbly with your God"? Why do you think the Lord requires these traits in his followers?

STUDY 3

LET JUSTICE ROLL

"Let justice roll on like a river, righteousness like a never-failing stream" (Amos 5:24) is one of the most quoted passages in the book of Amos. But what was really going on when the prophet proclaimed these words? The book is primarily a call to the people of Israel regarding their social injustice and their *apostasy*, or continuous turning away from God. Amos said that because of the people's actions, God's punishment was imminent and would not be pretty. These words are a cry from God through Amos, proclaiming that justice will come to Israel.

Amos outlines many of the transgressions the people have committed: mistreatment of the poor (see 5:11), afflictions against the righteous (see verse 7), receiving bribes (see verse 12), and being arrogant and complacent (see 6:1). Just like the other prophets of this time, and throughout the nation's history, he was holding the people accountable for their actions and reminding them that God had called them to a life of justice and righteousness.

Yet even with these words of warning, the prophet provided hope. Amos proclaimed that if the people turned to God, he would be merciful to the remnant left after the destruction and punishment that was coming in their day of judgment. The final verses of the book of Amos speak of hope, restoration, and repair: "I will restore David's fallen shelter—I will repair its broken walls and restore its ruins—and will rebuild it as it used to be" (Amos 9:11).

1. In many ways, Dr. Martin Luther King Jr. was in line with the prophet Amos when he warned America about some of its actions. What messages do you think Dr. King and Amos would proclaim today? What specific issues do you think they would speak out against?

> [13] "The days are coming," declares the LORD,
> "when the reaper will be overtaken by the plowman
> and the planter by the one treading grapes.
> New wine will drip from the mountains
> and flow from all the hills,
> [14] and I will bring my people Israel back from exile.
> "They will rebuild the ruined cities and live in them.
> They will plant vineyards and drink their wine;
> they will make gardens and eat their fruit.
> [15] I will plant Israel in their own land,
> never again to be uprooted
> from the land I have given them,"
> says the LORD your God (Amos 9:13–15).

2. What promise was God making to his people? How does the hope that God proclaims in this passage inspire your work of bringing justice to your world today? What messages can help you keep working toward justice in spite of the unjust issues around you?

3. How do you define *righteousness* and *justice* after going through this session? How has your understanding of these terms changed? How should this new understanding of righteousness and justice impact your actions in the work of racial reconciliation?

> ¹⁸ "The Spirit of the Lord is on me,
>   because he has anointed me
>   to proclaim good news to the poor.
> He has sent me to proclaim freedom for the prisoners
>   and recovery of sight for the blind,
> to set the oppressed free,
>   ¹⁹ to proclaim the year of the Lord's favor" (Luke 4:18–19).

4. Jesus spoke these words at the beginning of his ministry in the synagogue in his hometown of Nazareth. Why do you think it was important for Jesus to say that the Lord's Spirit was upon him? How is God's Spirit needed in your work for justice and righteousness?

5. What are some of the specific charges that Jesus mentions in these verses as a part of his mission on earth? What do these charges mean? How do they inform your work for justice?

CONNECT & CATCH UP

Take time today to connect with a fellow group member and discuss the key insights from this session. Use any of the following prompts to help guide your discussion.

What are the differences between retributive justice and restorative justice?

How did Jesus exemplify both forms of justice in his life, teaching, and ministry?

Why is the cornerstone of justice to remember that every human being is created in the image of God—the *imago dei* in Latin—and thus has inherent worth?

Where do you see your work intersecting with restorative justice? What help do you think you need to fulfill the work of restorative justice?

Use this time to go back and complete any of the study and reflection questions from previous days that you weren't able to finish. Make a note below of any revelations you've had and reflect on any growth or personal insights you've gained.

FREEDOM

So if the Son sets you free,
you will be free indeed.

JOHN 8:36

"From every mountainside, let **freedom** ring."

DR. MARTIN LUTHER KING JR.

WELCOME |

What does freedom look like? To one tired, overworked, forty-two-year-old woman, it looked like the ability to take a seat on a bus after she had paid her fare, made her way to her section, and settled in with her belongings. Rosa Parks's refusal to give up her seat to a white passenger on a Montgomery bus on December 1, 1955, was nothing less than a declaration of freedom.[20]

The civil rights movement sought to free people from injustices and discrimination. Rosa Parks's act—seeking to be free and live freely as she understood herself to be created by God—would go on to impact others' freedom as well. She demonstrated the words that Dr. King would later write in his *Letter from Birmingham City Jail*: "Freedom is never voluntarily given by the oppressor; it must be demanded by the oppressed."[21]

Despite the gains of the civil rights movement, freedom is still only a concept to some. Slavery exists in various forms, such as human trafficking and harsh labor conditions. On a spiritual level, it exists in the form of sin. When we submit to sin, we are shackled and face death (see Romans 6:23). However, through Jesus, we can be liberated from the chains of sin. We can live in freedom, knowing that we have been joined with Christ.

Our freedom from sin should compel us to want the same kind of freedom for others. Our witness of Jesus' liberation power testifies that *everyone* can be set free from bondage. We then join with God to liberate those who are not yet free, recognizing that freedom is woven into our human spirit. In the words of Dr. King, "To rob a man of freedom is to take from him the essential basis of his manhood . . . to rob him of something of God's image."[22]

CONNECT | 15 MINUTES

Get the session started by choosing one of these questions to discuss as a group:

- What is something that spoke to your heart in last week's personal study that you would like to share with the group?

  — *or* —

- Why does slavery of any form go against God's design for humans?

WATCH | 20 MINUTES

Now watch the video for this session. Below is an outline of the key points covered during the teaching. Record any thoughts or concepts that stand out to you.

OUTLINE

I. Throughout history and across cultures, freedom is recognized as a human right.
   A. *Freedom* can be defined as liberation from slavery or restraint.
   B. To take a person's freedom is to rob him of something of God's image.
   C. God etched in our hearts the desire for freedom.

II. We can draw lessons about freedom from the story of the Israelites in the Bible.
   A. The Israelites cried out to God under the weight of their slavery in Egypt.
   B. God heard their groaning and remembered the covenant that he had made with Abraham.
   C. God then sent Moses to deliver his people out of slavery and into freedom in the promised land.

III. People throughout the generations have been oppressed by spiritual slavery.
   A. Jesus is God's answer to our spiritual slavery.
   B. Jesus became our ransom—his life was the price for our freedom.
   C. Slavery breaks God's heart and opposes his will and design for humanity.

IV. African Americans have endured years of slavery and discrimination in the United States.
   A. From a historical perspective, slavery in America ended at the conclusion of the Civil War.
   B. But many wanted to deny African Americans their fundamental human rights of freedom.
   C. The civil rights movement sought to grant freedom and equal treatment to African Americans.

V. We need to act to give freedom to those who are in physical or spiritual slavery.
   A. It is estimated that forty million men, women, and children are in slavery today.
   B. There are three things we can do to help those who are enslaved today:
      1. Get educated about human trafficking today and spread the word.
      2. Say something if you notice a situation that seems off.
      3. Don't go it alone—there are many organizations that are working to stop human trafficking.

NOTES

_____

_____

_____

_____

_____

_____

_____

_____

_____

_____

_____

_____

_____

_____

_____

DISCUSS | 35 MINUTES

Discuss what you just watched by answering the following questions.

1. Rosa Parks's refusal to obey a discriminatory law led to the Montgomery bus boycott and sparked a movement that advocated for the rights for minorities in this country. What other small acts like this have you seen spark a movement? Why do you think these kinds of small acts can lead to larger movements?

2. When have you witnessed the restriction of another person's freedoms through either physical slavery, discrimination, or some other form? Describe what you witnessed and what happened. How do these kinds of restrictions oppose the person's humanity?

3. Slavery can be both physical and spiritual. Paul wrote, "When you offer yourselves to someone as obedient slaves, you are slaves of the one you obey—whether you are slaves to sin, which leads to death, or to obedience, which leads to righteousness" (Romans 6:16). What does it mean to be a slave to sin? How does a person find freedom?

4. Jesus taught, "A slave has no permanent place in the family, but a son belongs to it forever. So if the Son sets you free, you will be free indeed" (John 8:34–36). What is the difference between a slave and a son? How do Jesus' words inspire you to fight for freedom for those in bondage to sin and to physical oppressors?

5. There are three ways to bring justice to those enslaved: (1) get educated, (2) say something, and (3) don't go it alone. Why is it so important to follow these steps when you see a person who is being enslaved either physically or spiritually?

RESPOND | 10 MINUTES

Freedom is a biblical concept. All humans, created in the image and likeness of God (see Genesis 1:26), have an inherent desire for freedom. But part of walking in the freedom that God offers is learning to follow his commands. Read what the psalmist writes about this in the following passage in Psalm 119:41–48, and then answer the questions that follow.

> [41] May your unfailing love come to me, LORD,
>   your salvation, according to your promise;
> [42] then I can answer anyone who taunts me,
>   for I trust in your word.
> [43] Never take your word of truth from my mouth,
>   for I have put my hope in your laws.
> [44] I will always obey your law,
>   for ever and ever.
> [45] I will walk about in freedom,
>   for I have sought out your precepts.
> [46] I will speak of your statutes before kings
>   and will not be put to shame,
> [47] for I delight in your commands
>   because I love them.
> [48] I reach out for your commands, which I love,
>   that I may meditate on your decrees.

What connection does the psalmist make between following God's laws and living in freedom?

Do you "delight" in following God's commands? Why or why not?

PRAY | 10 MINUTES

End your time by praying for those who are physically enslaved by other humans and those who are enslaved to sin. Ask God to give you the boldness and courage you need to stand up to any instances of modern-day slavery that you confront. Close your time by using the space below to write down any requests so you can continue to pray about them in the week ahead.

Name   **Request**

PERSONAL STUDY

In the last personal study, you explored how Jesus modeled a broader definition of *justice* that includes both retributive and restorative justice and how God calls each of us to do the same. You looked at how being a person of restorative justice requires you to become the person who "puts right" the harms that have been done to others. In this week's personal study, you will examine how Jesus not only came into this broken world to bring restorative justice but also how he came to bring freedom to all who are held in spiritual bondage to the slavery of sin.

WHAT IS FREEDOM?

Freedom is more than a human right or desire. It's more than a principle that men and women have fought to obtain. Freedom is exactly what Jesus proclaimed that he came to give. At the start of his ministry, he stood in the synagogue in his hometown of Nazareth and, quoting from the prophet Isaiah, announced his mission statement: "The Spirit of the Lord is on me, because he has anointed me to proclaim good news to the poor. He has sent me to proclaim freedom for the prisoners and recovery of sight for the blind, to set the oppressed free" (Luke 4:18).

Jesus *represents* freedom, and Jesus *provides* freedom to all who accept his sacrifice and believe on him as the Son of God. As John famously wrote in his Gospel, "For God so loved the world that he gave his one and only Son, that whoever believes in him shall not perish but have eternal life" (John 3:16). Jesus came to bring freedom and "life . . . to the full" (John 10:10).

If we are not physically enslaved or do not witness such slavery on a regular basis, we may take the fundamental right of freedom for granted. We may not always think about what it means to be free and how this allows us to live according to our God-given purpose. But the reality is that "all have sinned and fall short of the glory of God" (Romans 3:23), and since "the wages of sin is death" (6:23), all of us need the freedom that Jesus came into this world to give.

[1] It is for freedom that Christ has set us free. Stand firm, then, and do not let yourselves be burdened again by a yoke of slavery. . . . [13] You, my brothers and sisters, were called to be free. But do not use your freedom to indulge the flesh; rather, serve one another humbly in love. [14] For the entire law is fulfilled in keeping this one command: "Love your neighbor as yourself." [15] If you bite and devour each other, watch out or you will be destroyed by each other. [16] So I say, walk by the Spirit, and you will not gratify the desires of the flesh (Galatians 5:1, 13–16).

1. Reflect on how you were in bondage to sin before you accepted Christ. What is the difference between living as a slave to sin and living free in Jesus? What difference have you seen in your life? What caution does Paul provide to followers of Christ in verse 1?

2. Paul shares in verses 13–16 how free brothers and sisters in Christ should live. How are we to use our freedom? What should be our guiding principle?

3. "If the Son sets you free, you will be free indeed" (John 8:36). From what has the Son set you free? How can you use this freedom to help liberate others?

8 Then a new king, to whom Joseph meant nothing, came to power in Egypt. 9 "Look," he said to his people, "the Israelites have become far too numerous for us. 10 Come, we must deal shrewdly with them or they will become even more numerous and, if war breaks out, will join our enemies, fight against us and leave the country" (Exodus 1:8–10).

A Definition of Freedom

What is freedom? It is, first, the capacity to deliberate or weigh alternatives. "Shall I be a teacher or lawyer?" "Shall I be a Democrat, Republican or Socialist?" Second, freedom expresses itself in decision. The word *decision* like the word *incision* involves the image of cutting. *Incision* means to cut in, *decision* means to cut off. When I make a decision I cut off alternatives and make a choice. The existentialists say we must choose; that we are choosing animals; and if we do not choose we sink into thinghood and the mass mind. A third expression of freedom is responsibility. This is the obligation of the person to respond if he is questioned about his decisions. No one else can respond for him. He alone must respond, for his acts are determined by the centered totality of his being.

From this analysis we can clearly see the evilness of segregation. It cuts off one's capacity to deliberate, decide and respond.

The absence of freedom is the imposition of restraint on my deliberation as to what I shall do, where I shall live, how much I shall earn, the kind of tasks I shall pursue. I am robbed of the basic quality of man-ness. When I cannot choose what I shall do or where I shall live or how I shall survive, it means in fact that someone or some system has already made these a pirori decisions for me, and I am reduced to an animal. I do not live; I merely exist. The only resemblances I have to real life are the motor responses and functions that are akin to humankind. I cannot adequately assume responsibility as a person because I have been made a party to a decision in which I played no part in making.

DR. MARTIN LUTHER KING JR.

FROM A SPEECH DELIVERED AT A CHURCH CONFERENCE
IN NASHVILLE, TENNESSEE, ON DECEMBER 27, 1962[23]

4. The Israelites had gone to Egypt to escape a famine in the land (see Genesis 46:3–7). How did the Israelites then become enslaved in Egypt? What fear did the king have concerning them? What do you think is the objective of those like the king who oppress others?

[11] But Moses said to God, "Who am I that I should go to Pharaoh and bring the Israelites out of Egypt?" [12] And God said, "I will be with you. And this will be the sign to you that it is I who have sent you: When you have brought the people out of Egypt, you will worship God on this mountain." [13] Moses said to God, "Suppose I go to the Israelites and say to them, 'The God of your fathers has sent me to you,' and they ask me, 'What is his name?' Then what shall I tell them?" [14] God said to Moses, "I AM WHO I AM. This is what you are to say to the Israelites: 'I AM has sent me to you'" (Exodus 3:11–14).

5. God called up Moses to lead the Israelites to freedom. What objections did Moses have about speaking out about Pharaoh's oppression? What objections have you raised about your role in speaking out against injustice? How might God be speaking to you about your objections?

STUDY 2
YOKED TO JESUS

When we hear the word *yoke,* we often think of it as a metaphor for service or bondage. The word is used in Scripture many times, often with that symbolism implied (see 1 Kings 12:4; Isaiah 9:4; Jeremiah 5:5), though at other times just to refer to a wooden apparatus placed over the necks of animals for pulling a plow or cart (see 1 Samuel 6:7; 1 Kings 19:19). Animals were typically required to pull heavy weights, and so the yoke distributed the weight more equally so that both animals (or the team of animals) were sharing the burden of the load.

In the same way, when people are yoked together, they walk together, bearing each other's burdens and sharing the heavy load or weight of the issues. We are actually commanded in Scripture to "carry each other's burdens" in this manner (Galatians 6:2) and are warned against being "yoked together with unbelievers" (2 Corinthians 6:14).

However, in one of Jesus' teachings, a slightly different image comes to mind when we hear him use the word *yoke.* Jesus actually instructs us to take his yoke on ourselves and to learn from him. He says that his yoke is easy, which stands in stark opposition to the image of animals carrying a heavy load. Even more, Jesus says that we will receive rest when we take up his yoke! The image of heaviness and hard labor is replaced with a lightness and invitation to live more easily and freely. Jesus' yoke, indeed, offers a different way of living and being.

> [25] At that time Jesus said, "I praise you, Father, Lord of heaven and earth, because you have hidden these things from the wise and learned, and revealed them to little children. [26] Yes, Father, for this is what you were pleased to do. [27] All things have been committed to me by my Father. No one knows the Son except the Father, and no one knows the Father except the Son and those to whom the Son chooses to reveal him. [28] Come to me, all you who are weary and burdened, and I will give you rest. [29] Take my yoke upon you and learn from me, for I am gentle and humble in heart, and you will find rest for your souls. [30] For my yoke is easy and my burden is light" (Matthew 11:25–30).

1. Jesus begins this teaching on taking up his "yoke" with a prayer to his heavenly Father. What does Jesus say that God has revealed to those who seek him?

2. Look at the invitation Jesus gives to those who are "weary and burdened" (verse 28). What images come to mind when you hear Jesus speak of his yoke?

3. Jesus states he is "gentle and humble in heart" (verse 29). Why do you think he added this remark? What does this say about the kind of yoke he offers to us?

4. What are some ways you invite others to choose freedom and be yoked to Jesus? What can you do this week to share the freedom of Christ? Who will you share it with?

5. One commentator translates verse 30 in this way: "Keep company with me and you'll learn to live freely and lightly."[24] What does this imply about finding freedom in *walking* with Christ? Why is it important to always stay in step with Christ to experience freedom?

The Goal Is Freedom

Freedom is like life. You cannot be given life in installments. You cannot be given breath but no body, nor a heart but no blood vessels. Freedom is one thing—you have it all, or you are not free.

Our goal is freedom. I believe we will win it because the goal of the nation is freedom. Yet we are not passively waiting for a deliverance to come from others moved by their pity for us. Our destiny is bound up with the destiny of America—we built it for two centuries without wages, we made cotton king, we built our houses and homes for our masters and suffered injustice and humiliation—but out of a bottomless vitality continued to live and grow. If the inexpressible cruelties of slavery could not extinguish our existence, the opposition we now face will surely fall. We feel that we are the conscience of America—we are its troubled soul—we will continue to insist that right be done because both God's will and the heritage of our nation speak through our echoing demands.

We are simply seeking to bring into full realization the American dream—a dream yet unfulfilled. A dream of equality of opportunity, of privilege and property widely distributed; a dream of a land where men no longer argue that the color of a man's skin determines the content of his character; the dream of a land where every man will respect the dignity and worth of human personality—this is the dream. When it is realized, the jangling discords of our nation will be transformed into a beautiful symphony of brotherhood, and men everywhere will know that America is truly the land of the free and the home of the brave.

DR. MARTIN LUTHER KING JR.

FROM AN ADDRESS BEFORE THE NATIONAL PRESS CLUB
IN WASHINGTON, DC, ON JULY 19, 1962[25]

STUDY 3
SET OTHERS FREE

Once the Israelites had been delivered from bondage in Egypt and were entering into the promised land, the Lord gave them certain rules and regulations they were to follow. These laws instructed the Israelites on how to live as his people and were intended to help them avoid falling into idolatry—another form of bondage. God wanted his people to be free.

God gave his people specific guidelines on how to treat each other as well as the land. One of these laws the Lord instituted was the Year of Jubilee, which was to take place every forty-nine years (see Leviticus 25:8). During this Year of Jubilee—or year of freedom—the people were to return to their own property (see verse 13), be released from their debts (see verses 23–28), and freed from all types of bondage (see verses 39–55). They were to remember the land belonged to the Lord and they resided there as strangers (see verse 23).

The passage lists other ways God's people were to treat each other, but the common thread and theme that runs throughout is fairness and care. Both the land and God's people were to be treated fairly and with care. We can infer from this that freedom equals fairness and care. When we take care of each other, we grant freedom to them. We chose not to rule over them with brute force, but instead we fear God and treat those made in his image with care.

> [13] "In this Year of Jubilee everyone is to return to their own property. [14] If you sell land to any of your own people or buy land from them, do not take advantage of each other. [15] You are to buy from your own people on the basis of the number of years since the Jubilee. And they are to sell to you on the basis of the number of years left for harvesting crops. [16] When the years are many, you are to increase the price, and when the years are few, you are to decrease the price, because what is really being sold to you is the number of crops. [17] Do not take advantage of each other, but fear your God. I am the LORD your God" (Leviticus 25:13–17).

1. When the Israelites came into the promised land, the territory was allotted according to tribes and families. These initial tracts were to be returned to the original owners on the Year of Jubilee. How would this system have ensured that no family or tribe would forever be without land? How would this have contributed to the people's freedom?

2. Twice God says to "not take advantage of each other" (verses 14, 17). Why do you think he stressed this point? How is care and fairness a recurring theme throughout this passage?

> 39 "If any of your fellow Israelites become poor and sell themselves to you, do not make them work as slaves. 40 They are to be treated as hired workers or temporary residents among you; they are to work for you until the Year of Jubilee. 41 Then they and their children are to be released, and they will go back to their own clans and to the property of their ancestors. 42 Because the Israelites are my servants, whom I brought out of Egypt, they must not be sold as slaves" (Leviticus 25:39–42).

3. It was common in the ancient world for those in poverty to sell themselves into slavery to pay their debts. (In many cases, the only alternative was starvation.) But God wanted something different and better for his people. How were the poor to be treated?

4. Why do you think God instituted a Year of Jubilee? Why do you think he was so detailed in how the people were to act? What does this show us about how God values freedom?

5. What differences would we see in our world today if we followed the principles outlined in Leviticus 25? What can you do to bring about fairness and care?

CONNECT & CATCH UP

Take time today to connect with a fellow group member and discuss the key insights from this session. Use any of the following prompts to help guide your discussion.

Slavery is directly opposed to God's will and design for humanity. How does the story of the Israelites in Egypt reveal that slavery and bondage breaks his heart?

Based on your reflections from this week, how do you define freedom?

Do you believe freedom is everyone's right? Why or why not?

How does the freedom that you have received in Christ encourage you to work for freedom for others?

Use this time to go back and complete any of the study and reflection questions from previous days that you weren't able to finish. Make a note below of any revelations you've had and reflect on any growth or personal insights you've gained.

PERSEVERANCE

Therefore, since we are surrounded by such a great cloud of witnesses, let us throw off everything that hinders and the sin that so easily entangles. And let us run with perseverance the race marked out for us.

HEBREWS 12:1

"I am not **unmindful** that some of you have come here out of great **trials** and **tribulations**."

Dr. Martin Luther King Jr.

WELCOME

On April 10, 1960, Dr. King gave a speech at Spelman College in Atlanta, Georgia. In his address, he encouraged the students to persevere and keep fighting for justice—especially within the student movement that was sweeping through the nation at the time. He ended his speech with a now famous quote: "If you can't fly, run; if you can't run, walk; if you can't walk, crawl; but by all means keep moving."

When we grow weary, our first response is to want to give up. When our goals seem far away—perhaps as far away as a mountain top—our resolve can wane. We no longer have the energy, will, or stamina to even want to fly. But it is at these times we need to keep moving forward—regardless of whether those steps are great or small. We can't give up. We may not always fly, but that doesn't mean we can't crawl. By whatever means we have, we need to keep moving. This is the essence of perseverance.

Those in the civil rights movement had to develop perseverance to travel the long road toward justice. They grew tired. They felt uncertain of the way ahead. They grew discouraged at the lack of progress. Even Dr. King admitted, "Living every day under the threat of death, I feel discouraged sometimes. Living every day under extensive criticisms . . . I feel discouraged sometimes. Yes, sometimes I feel discouraged and feel my work's in vain." But then he added, "Then the Holy Spirit revives my soul again."[26]

In this session, we will explore what it takes to have perseverance—not only as we see it in the civil rights movement but in any movement that seeks to bring about justice. We will find that if we do "not become weary in doing good . . . at the proper time we will reap a harvest" (Galatians 6:9). *Perseverance* is key as we work together to share the dream.

CONNECT | 15 MINUTES

Get the session started by choosing one of these questions to discuss as a group:

- What is something that spoke to your heart in last week's personal study that you would like to share with the group?

  — *or* —

- Why is perseverance a needed characteristic when working for justice?

WATCH | 20 MINUTES

Now watch the video for this session. Below is an outline of the key points covered during the teaching. Record any thoughts or concepts that stand out to you.

OUTLINE

I. Perseverance has long been a characteristic of African Americans' fight for racial equality in the United States.
   A. Segregation was legalized in the South under the Jim Crow laws.
   B. The civil rights movement was born to regain basic rights for African Americans and minorities living in the United States.
   C. But African Americans had been fighting for their rights for decades before the movement began.
II. The quiet middle of the civil rights movement is marked by perseverance.
   A. *Perseverance* can be defined as "active persistence."
   B. Perseverance is different from *patience* in that perseverance does something.
   C. We are to "run with perseverance the race marked out for us" (Hebrews 12:1).
III. It is challenging to run the race of perseverance when we face trials and opposition.
   A. Dr. King and others in the movement grew discouraged but never resigned to the status quo.
   B. Jesus encourages us to "take heart" in trials because he has "overcome the world" (John 16:33).
   C. We can even rejoice when we "face trials" because it "produces perseverance" in us (James 1:2–3).
IV. There are many people today who are persevering in the quest for justice.
   A. Maedeh Hojabri led a campaign against laws forcing Iranian women to wear head coverings.
   B. Manal al-Sharif challenged polices that discriminate against women in Saudi Arabia.
   C. While challenges still exist, these women and others persevere for major legal changes.
V. How can we actively persist on behalf of freedom and justice?
   A. We need to speak up and act against any injustice that we see in our communities.
   B. We must also take the matter to God and persist in prayer (see Luke 18:1–8).
   C. As people of faith, we can persevere because we know that we *will* overcome.

NOTES

DISCUSS | 35 MINUTES

Discuss what you just watched by answering the following questions.

1. Individuals like Dr. Martin Luther King Jr. and Rosa Parks were "runners" in a race for equality that had started long before them. What part did perseverance play in the overarching story of the civil rights movement?

2. The words *patience* and *perseverance* are sometimes used interchangeably. How would you describe the difference between them? Why are *both* needed to fight injustice?

3. Jesus said, "In this world you will have trouble. But take heart! I have overcome the world" (John 16:33). Perseverance is needed in this life because troubles come with life. But what promise does Jesus give in this verse? How can this help you persevere as you take action against injustices in your community?

4. Jesus told his disciples the parable of the persistent widow "to show them that they should always pray and not give up" (Luke 18:1). What does the parable reveal about the power of perseverance not only in prayer but also in taking concrete action for just causes?

5. There are many examples of people persevering in the face of injustice—men and women like Iranian activist Maedeh Hojabri and Saudi Arabian activist Manal al-Sharif. But what stories do you feel God is calling *you* to step into when it comes to fighting injustice? What opportunities do you see to persevere on behalf of others in your community?

RESPOND | 10 MINUTES

It is easy to get discouraged when we are pursuing a goal and encounter setbacks along the way. However, the Bible instructs us to not lose sight of the fact that the trials we face are actually shaping our character and developing us into stronger and more confident people. Read what Paul and James write about this below, and then answer the questions that follow.

> [3] Not only so, but we also glory in our sufferings, because we know that suffering produces perseverance; [4] perseverance, character; and character, hope. [5] And hope does not put us to shame, because God's love has been poured out into our hearts through the Holy Spirit, who has been given to us (Romans 5:3-5).
>
> [2] Consider it pure joy, my brothers and sisters, whenever you face trials of many kinds, [3] because you know that the testing of your faith produces perseverance. [4] Let perseverance finish its work so that you may be mature and complete, not lacking anything (James 1:2-4).

Compare and contrast what is being said in these passages. What do both Paul and James say followers of Christ should do when they face trials and even suffering?

What do Paul and James say about the value of persevering through trials?

PRAY | 10 MINUTES

End your meeting by praying together as a group. Use this time to share any challenges you are experiencing as it relates to the core concepts of love, conscience, justice, freedom, and perseverance that you have been discussing in this study. Close your time by writing down any prayer requests mentioned in the space below so you can pray about them in the week ahead.

Name   **Request**

PERSONAL STUDY

In the previous personal study, you looked at the principle of *freedom* and how it is God's plan and purpose for every person to not be enslaved by either another person or by the shackles of sin. You explored how God freed his people from bondage in Egypt and the laws he instituted to make sure his people lived in freedom. In this session, you looked at how pursuing justice and freedom for others is often a long process . . . and one that always requires *perseverance*.

STUDY 1

WHAT IS PERSEVERANCE?

When we get tired, it can be challenging for us to stay focused on a goal. We get weighed down by the issues at hand and wonder how long it will take for any positive outcomes to occur. Weariness is an enemy of progress that tempts us to give in and throw in the towel. This is especially true after experiencing a setback.

In 1961, activists formed the Albany Movement to protest racial segregation in the city of Albany, Georgia. But the police chief effectively jailed protestors and stalled the movement. Dr. King arrived in the city in December to reinvigorate the campaign and bring in some much-needed media attention, but by the end of the movement in 1962, all of the city's public facilities remained segregated.[27]

Such defeats can cause us to ask, *Why are we working so hard with no results? Why are we even trying to bring about change? What's the point?* We might even wonder if change is possible. But as Dr. King would later say at a speech in Washington, DC, "We must accept finite disappointment, but never lose infinite hope."[28]

There is hope for the weary soul. When we encounter seasons of doubt and weariness and are tempted to give up, we must focus on the example of Christ, who "endured the cross, scorning its shame" (Hebrews 12:2). Renewing our minds, reviewing our goals, and reminding ourselves of Jesus' words will encourage us to persevere and keep moving until we overcome.

> [1] Therefore, since we are surrounded by such a great cloud of witnesses, let us throw off everything that hinders and the sin that so easily entangles. And let us run with perseverance the race marked out for us, [2] fixing our eyes on Jesus, the pioneer and perfecter of faith. For the joy set before him he endured the cross, scorning its shame, and sat down at the right hand of the throne of God. [3] Consider him who endured such opposition from sinners, so that you will not grow weary and lose heart (Hebrews 12:1-3).

1. The author of this passage pictures the Christian life as a race that must be run. As is true of any race, the participants must stay engaged and focused on the ultimate goal of reaching the finish line in order to stay motivated. What are you to fix your eyes on as you run? What practices help you see Jesus and remind you to draw strength from him?

2. What are some other things a marathon runner has to do to complete a 26.2-mile race? How can some of these actions relate to the spiritual "race" and the fight for justice?

3. What are some of the things that are hindering you right now in your fight against injustice? What may entangle you and cause you not to work?

4. The author of this passage points out that Jesus was willing to persevere and endure even the scorn of the cross to achieve his ultimate goal of restoration between God and humankind. How can this inspire you to persevere as you pursue your goals?

5. In James 4:8, we read, "Come near to God and he will come near to you." What ways can you draw closer to God today? How might this help you persevere?

Not the Way Out

In every movement toward freedom, some of the oppressed prefer to remain oppressed. Almost twenty-eight hundred years ago, Moses set out to lead the children of Israel from the slavery of Egypt to the freedom of the promised land. He soon discovered that slaves do not always welcome their deliverers. They become accustomed to being slaves. They would rather bear those ills they have . . . than flee to others that they know not of. They prefer the "fleshpots of Egypt" to the ordeals of emancipation.

There is such a thing as the freedom from exhaustion. Some people are so worn down by the yoke of oppression that they give up. A few years ago in the slum areas of Atlanta, a Negro guitarist used to sing almost daily: "Been down so long that down don't bother me." This is the type of negative freedom and resignation that often engulfs the life of the oppressed.

But this is not the way out. To accept passively an unjust system is to cooperate with that system; thereby the oppressed become as evil as the oppressor. Noncooperation with evil is as much a moral obligation as is cooperation with good. The oppressed must never allow the conscience of the oppressor to slumber. Religion reminds every man that he is his brother's keeper. To accept injustice or segregation passively is to say to the oppressor that his actions are morally right. . . . So acquiescence—while often the easier way—is not the moral way.

DR. MARTIN LUTHER KING JR.

FROM *STRIDE TOWARD FREEDOM*, A MEMOIR FROM
DR. KING ABOUT THE MONTGOMERY BUS BOYCOTT,
PUBLISHED ON SEPTEMBER 17, 1958[29]

STUDY 2

VALUE PERSEVERANCE

The word *perseverance* might bring up mixed emotions for you. It may remind you that "in this world you will have trouble," as Jesus mentioned to his disciples in John 16:33. It can bring to mind the situation of Paul, who for the sake of the gospel was "hard pressed on every side . . . perplexed . . . persecuted . . . struck down" (2 Corinthians 4:8–9). No one welcomes trouble. But persevering through trials does have value.

As you explored during this week's group time, James makes this assertion when he states, "Consider it pure joy, my brothers and sisters, whenever you face trials of many kinds, because you know that the testing of your faith produces perseverance. Let perseverance finish its work so that you may be mature and complete, not lacking anything" (James 1:2–4).

While *joy* may not be your first response to troubles, understanding this biblical mindset can help you put your trials into perspective and recognize that some good will come out of them—that those difficulties you are enduring will produce much-needed fruit in your life. When you view your trials in this way, it inspires and encourages you to keep pushing through them. Instead of focusing on what is hard, you focus on what is happening in you.

So stay alert and in tune with God. Keep track of the ways you are growing as you are exposed to possibilities. Look out for the good things that perseverance is producing in you.

> ³ Not only so, but we also glory in our sufferings, because we know that suffering produces perseverance; ⁴ perseverance, character; and character, hope. ⁵ And hope does not put us to shame, because God's love has been poured out into our hearts through the Holy Spirit, who has been given to us (Romans 5:3–5).

1. You looked at this passage during your group time, but take a moment to again consider these traits that Paul lists. Write out how each characteristic produces another one.

   Suffering:

   Perseverance:

   Character:

   Hope:

2. Now write out how you've seen a trial develop these characteristics in you or someone else.

   Suffering:

   Perseverance:

   Character:

   Hope:

[5] For this very reason, make every effort to add to your faith goodness; and to goodness, knowledge; [6] and to knowledge, self-control; and to self-control, perseverance; and to perseverance, godliness; [7] and to godliness, mutual affection; and to mutual affection, love. [8] For if you possess these qualities in

increasing measure, they will keep you from being ineffective and unproductive in your knowledge of our Lord Jesus Christ. [9] But whoever does not have them is nearsighted and blind, forgetting that they have been cleansed from their past sins (2 Peter 1:5–9).

3. Peter lists several more qualities in this passage that develop out of perseverance. Which of these benefits have you personally experienced because you persevered through a trial?

4. What is the value of possessing "these qualities in increasing measure" (verse 8)? What happens if you do not gain these qualities in your walk with Christ?

5. As you reflect on these passages, what would you say is the greatest benefit that persevering through troubles has produced in your life?

Continue
the Struggle

Now it is true, if I may speak figuratively, that Old Man Segregation is on his deathbed. But history has proven that social systems have a great last-minute breathing power, and the guardians of the status quo are always on hand with their oxygen tents to keep the old order alive. Segregation is still a fact in America. We still confront it in the South in its glaring and conspicuous forms. We still confront it in the North in its hidden and subtle forms. But if democracy is to live, segregation must die.

Segregation is a glaring evil. It is utterly unchristian. It relegates the segregated to the status of a thing rather than elevates him to the status of a person. Segregation is nothing but slavery covered up with certain niceties of complexity. Segregation is a blatant denial of the unity which we all have in Christ Jesus. So we must continue the struggle against segregation in order to speed up the coming of the inevitable. . . .

Wherever we find segregation, we must have the fortitude to passively resist it. I realize that this will mean suffering and sacrifice. It might even mean going to jail. If such is the case we must be willing to fill up the jail houses of the South. It might even mean physical death. But if physical death is the price that some must pay to free their children from a permanent life of psychological death, then nothing could be more honorable. Once more it might turn out that the blood of the martyr will be the seed of the tabernacle of freedom.

DR. MARTIN LUTHER KING JR.

FROM AN ADDRESS AT THE FIRST ANNUAL INSTITUTE
ON NON-VIOLENCE AND SOCIAL CHANGE IN
MONTGOMERY, ALABAMA, IN DECEMBER 1956[30]

STUDY 3

WE WILL OVERCOME

Jesus never said that life would be easy. In fact, he assured us that "in this world [we] will have trouble" (John 16:33). Jesus knew that things would get challenging for his disciples after his ascension, and he knew that things would get challenging for us today. Yet within his message about trouble he encouraged us to "take heart." His words were not based on a feel-good message but on the truth. He has overcome the world. Trouble won't last. We *will* overcome.

Focusing on this truth can give us the hope and perspective we need to overcome the many trials of this life. After all, if Jesus overcame the world, surely he can give us all that is needed to be overcomers as well. Paul also reminds us that we have "incomparably great power," which is the same as "the mighty strength he [God] exerted when he raised Christ from the dead and seated him at his right hand in the heavenly realms" (Ephesians 1:19–20).

The reason we persevere is because we know God has called us to do what is right (see Micah 6:8). And we know that with God, we can overcome whatever difficulties, injustices, or troubles we face. So when confronted with the choice of giving up or pushing through, remember Jesus' words and keep going. You *are* able to overcome—and you *will* overcome if you don't give up. When you have God's power, all things are possible (see Matthew 19:26).

> 2 "In a certain town there was a judge who neither feared God nor cared what people thought. 3 And there was a widow in that town who kept coming to him with the plea, 'Grant me justice against my adversary.' 4 For some time he refused. But finally he said to himself, 'Even though I don't fear God or care what people think, 5 yet because this widow keeps bothering me, I will see that she gets justice, so that she won't eventually come and attack me!'" (Luke 18:2–5).

1. The judge in this parable could not be considered just because he "neither feared God nor cared what people thought" (verse 2). He had no desire to grant the widow justice. But what eventually caused him to relent and change his mind?

2. We often think of perseverance as something we do for a season. We commit to praying for an amount of time . . . but not necessarily until we see the resolution. What does this parable imply about how long the widow persevered?

> [6] And the Lord said, "Listen to what the unjust judge says. [7] And will not God bring about justice for his chosen ones, who cry out to him day and night? Will he keep putting them off? [8] I tell you, he will see that they get justice, and quickly. However, when the Son of Man comes, will he find faith on the earth?" (Luke 18:6–8).

3. How does God compare to the unjust judge in this parable? What does this say about God's desire to bring about justice to his children? What part does perseverance play in this?

4. What disciplines could you put into practice as a result of the message in this parable? How will you remember to consistently be persistent?

5. Think about your goals for justice—what you would like to see happen in relation to reconciliation and what part you would like to play. What are some action steps you could take to work toward those goals? How will you commit to staying dedicated to reaching those goals until you see them realized?

CONNECT & CATCH UP

Take time today to connect with a fellow group member and discuss the key insights from this session. Use any of the following prompts to help guide your discussion.

The time that Dr. King was involved in the civil rights movement was just the movement's *last* chapter. What are some of the ways that people persevered in the movement before him?

What types of things cause you to get the most weary when you are pursuing a cause for Christ?

What promise do we receive in Scripture if we remain faithful and persevere?

What are some practices you can follow when you are tempted to give up?

Use this time to go back and complete any of the study and reflection questions from previous days that you weren't able to finish. Make a note below of any revelations you've had and reflect on any growth or personal insights you've gained.

SESSION SIX

HOPE

Now faith is confidence in what we hope for and assurance about what we do not see.

HEBREWS 11:1

"With this **faith**, we will be able to hew out of the mountain of despair a **stone of hope.**"

DR. MARTIN LUTHER KING JR.

From the time Dr. King was recruited as spokesperson for the Montgomery bus boy-cott in 1955 until his assassination in 1968, he was a drum major for change. He marched, rallied, and stood up for what he believed was right. This fight wasn't an easy one, yet many accomplishments were realized during those thirteen years in Dr. King's life—and even in the years after his death. For instance, the Civil Rights Act, passed in 1964, made discrimination illegal in the United States. The Voting Rights Act, passed in 1965, prohibited barriers to voting that had been prevalent to stop blacks from voting.

Consider also that Dr. King's birthday became a national holiday in 1983, and by 2000, all fifty states had made the day a government holiday. This achievement was no small feat. As a federal holiday, people are prompted to stop and reflect on the life of Dr. King and the ideals he pursued. An entire nation pauses on the third Monday of each January to think about the works of the young minister born in 1929 in the segregated South.

Ironically, Dr. King shared a powerful thought the day before his death when he said, "Only when it is dark enough can you see the stars." His words spoke to the dark world around him and still speaks to the world around us today—a world filled with injustices, disparities, discrimination, and the like. Darkness hangs over our lives in this country as well as in the world. Yet those who subscribe to hope understand that darkness is an *opportunity*. It is the perfect setting for light to penetrate and illuminate desolate situations.

God has allowed us to live in this time. It isn't a surprise to him that we are in the midst of the troubles we are seeing. In fact, he has equipped us to participate in the solutions to those problems. It's up to us to see the opportunity and forge ahead with hope as we seek to bring about God's kingdom. It's up to us to move forward and shine the light.

CONNECT | 15 MINUTES

Get the session started by choosing one of these questions to discuss as a group:

- What is something that spoke to your heart in last week's personal study that you would like to share with the group?

  — *or* —

- Why is hope such a powerful force when it comes to confronting darkness?

WATCH | 20 MINUTES

Now watch the video for this session. Below is an outline of the key points covered during the teaching. Record any thoughts or concepts that stand out to you.

OUTLINE

I. It is only when the night is dark enough that we can see the stars of hope.
  A. Dr. King never gave up hope that one day racial equality would be realized in America.
  B. The story of Esther reveals that God can put us in a place "for such a time as this" (Esther 4:14).
  C. We are living in a dark-night season—but *God* has chosen us to live at this time.
II. When the night is dark, we have the choice of focusing on hope or despair.
  A. Biblical *hope* means "an indication of certainty" or a "strong and confident expectation."
  B. Throughout history, God's people have hoped for what he has promised but has not done yet.
  C. Israel hoped for deliverance from slavery in Egypt, from exile in Babylon, and for the coming of the Messiah—and each time, God delivered on his promise.
III. History reveals many other instances of hope giving birth to different human rights movements.
  A. Mahatma Gandhi practiced nonviolent resistance in South Africa in 1906.
  B. The Jews formed resistance groups during World War II and forced Nazi soldiers to retreat.
  C. Hope is about knowing that what you are doing will ultimately make a difference for good.
IV. Dark nights exist around the world today . . . but we can bring about hope.
  A. North Korea has been cut off from the world—will we hope on behalf of its people?
  B. The gap between rich and poor continues to grow—will we dare to hope for a solution?
  C. Our hope isn't *theoretical* but *certain* that one day the dignity of humans will be restored.
  D. Giving our time and resources to the cause of justice pushes out the darkness.
  E. Christ in us is truly the hope of the world.

NOTES

_____

_____

_____

_____

_____

_____

_____

_____

_____

_____

_____

_____

_____

_____

DISCUSS | 35 MINUTES

Discuss what you just watched by answering the following questions.

1. The night before Dr. King was assassinated, he gave a speech at Mason Temple in Memphis, Tennessee, in which he said, "Trouble is in the land; confusion all around . . . but I know, somehow, that only when it is dark enough can you see the stars." How do you think Dr. King was able to maintain his hope-filled perspective in spite of the threats he was facing?

2. Ask someone in the group to read aloud Esther 4:9–16. In this story, the Jewish people were facing annihilation at the hands of Haman, an official in the Persian government. The only hope the Jewish people had was that Esther, the queen, would be able to convince her husband, the king, to stop the slaughter. What did Mordecai say to Esther to convince her to act? What was Esther ultimately willing to do to obtain the king's justice for her people?

3. The Hebrew and Greek definitions of *hope* found in Scripture reveal that it is an "indication of certainty" and a "strong and confident expectation." How do these definitions help you understand the concept of hope? How is the reality of waiting inherent in these definitions?

4. The author of Hebrews states that "faith is confidence in what we hope for and assurance about what we do not see" (Hebrews 11:1). How has this kind of confident hope in God sustained you personally? How have you seen this kind of hope impact your community?

5. Jesus told his followers, "Let your light shine before others, that they may see your good deeds and glorify your Father in heaven" (Matthew 5:16). What areas do you consider dark in your community and world? How might you be a light in the midst of that darkness?

RESPOND | 10 MINUTES

The Bible instructs us to "not fear" (Isaiah 41:10), "not lose heart" (2 Corinthians 4:16), and "watch in hope for the LORD" (Micah 7:7). Several psalms also share this theme of placing our hope in God and trusting in him for deliverance. Read the following passage from Psalm 33:17–22, focusing on the phrases that include the word *hope*, and then answer the questions that follow.

> ¹⁷ A horse is a vain hope for deliverance;
>   despite all its great strength it cannot save.
> ¹⁸ But the eyes of the LORD are on those who fear him,
>   on those whose hope is in his unfailing love,
> ¹⁹ to deliver them from death
>   and keep them alive in famine.
> ²⁰ We wait in hope for the LORD;
>   he is our help and our shield.
> ²¹ In him our hearts rejoice,
>   for we trust in his holy name.
> ²² May your unfailing love be with us, LORD,
>   even as we put our hope in you.

What does the psalmist say about basing your hope on human means—such as horses or chariots in his day—for deliverance?

Based on these verses, how would you describe the word *hope*? How can you use these verses to help you continue to place your trust in God?

PRAY | 10 MINUTES

Conclude this session with a time of praise, thanking God for the insights you've gained during the course of this study. You may want to go around the room and hear what each member has taken away and what they intend to do going forward. Use the space below to write down any praise reports or prayer requests so you can continue to pray about them in the weeks ahead.

Name   **Request**

PERSONAL STUDY

Congratulations! You have reached the final personal study. Over the past few weeks, you have looked at several biblical principles that shaped Dr. King's belief in God and compelled him to stand up for those who were oppressed—*love, conscience, justice, freedom,* and *perseverance.* This week, you explored *hope,* which reminds us that our perspective in the midst of the darkness matters. Not only do we anticipate a positive outcome when fighting for others, but we rely on our faith and hope in Jesus' promise to bring about the victory. In this final session, we will focus on the value of hope as we persevere in our fight for justice.

WHAT IS HOPE?

We may think of hope as a desire or wishful thinking. We hope for many things: to get into the school we desire, to get the promotion, to get the good parking spot. In this context, hope *is* a wish or a desire. It's what we want to happen or want to have. Yet from a Christian perspective, hope is much more. Hope means certainty or strong and confident expectation. It's a guiding principle when pursuing justice and is a strong statement of faith in an almighty God.

The prophet Isaiah wrote, "Even youths grow tired and weary, and young men stumble and fall; but those who hope in the LORD will renew their strength. They will soar on wings like eagles; they will run and not grow weary, they will walk and not be faint" (Isaiah 40:30-31). The hope that God offers is more powerful than a mere wish. Our hope in the Lord not only renews our strength but also gives us supernatural strength to "soar on wings like eagles."

The biblical concept implies trust and confidence in God. Hope in the fight for justice is rooted in the same confidence. As justice seekers, we place our hope in God, anticipating his desired outcome. We align our actions with his will to produce what is right. We also understand that hope always implies *waiting*. What we anticipate has not already arrived—it is still on the way—and we are called to work with God to bring it about.

> [1] Now faith is confidence in what we hope for and assurance about what we do not see. [2] This is what the ancients were commended for. [3] By faith we understand that the universe was formed at God's command, so that what is seen was not made out of what was visible (Hebrews 11:1-3).

1. How is faith defined in this passage? As Christians, what are we hoping for? How does that shape our faith and our actions?

> [11] Therefore, remember that formerly you who are Gentiles by birth and called "uncircumcised" by those who call themselves "the circumcision" (which is done in the body by human hands)— [12] remember that at that time you were separate from Christ, excluded from citizenship in Israel and foreigners to the covenants of the promise, without hope and without God in the world. [13] But now in Christ Jesus you who once were far away have been brought near by the blood of Christ (Ephesians 2:11-13).

2. What were we before we accepted Jesus as our Savior? How were we without hope? What changed now—and how?

3. Based on these verses and your experience, how is a person hopeless without Christ? How does Christ bring hope? How can this hope fuel you to work for justice even in dark times?

> [7] Be still before the LORD and wait patiently for him; do not fret when people succeed in their ways, when they carry out their wicked schemes. [8] Refrain from anger and turn from wrath; do not fret—it leads only to evil. [9] For those who are evil will be destroyed, but those who hope in the LORD will inherit the land (Psalm 37:7-9).

4. When have you read about or observed a group of people wait, or hope, for deliverance? What did they do? How did they wait (or hope)? What happened?

5. Why is it so hard not to "fret" when you are waiting for God to provide? What is the promise for those who choose to wait and put their hope in the Lord?

The Last Word

A genuine revolution of values means, in the final analysis, that our loyalties must become ecumenical rather than sectional. Every nation must now develop an overriding loyalty to mankind as a whole in order to preserve the best in their individual societies. This call for a worldwide fellowship that lifts neighborly concern beyond one's tribe, race, class and nation is, in reality, a call for an all-embracing and unconditional love. This often misunderstood and misinterpreted concept has now become an absolute necessity for the survival of man.

When I speak of love, I am speaking of that force which all the great religions have seen as the supreme unifying principle of life. Love is the key that unlocks the door which leads to ultimate reality . . . beautifully summed up in the First Epistle of Saint John: "Let us love one another: for love is of God: and every one that loveth is born of God, and knoweth God. He that loveth not knoweth not God; for God is love. . . . If we love one another, God dwelleth in us, and his love is perfected in us."

Let us hope that this spirit will become the order of the day. We can no longer afford to worship the God of hate or bow before the altar of retaliation. As Arnold Toynbee once said in a speech: "Love is the ultimate force that makes for the saving choice of life and good against the damning choice of death and evil. Therefore the first hope in our inventory must be the hope that love is going to have the last word."

Dr. Martin Luther King Jr.

FROM *WHERE DO WE GO FROM HERE*, THE FINAL BOOK WRITTEN BY DR. KING BEFORE HIS ASSASSINATION, PUBLISHED IN 1967[31]

STUDY 2

CALLED TO BE LIGHTS

"Only when it is dark enough can you see the stars." This analogy from Dr. King echoes what Jesus said about "shining our light" to others: "A town built on a hill cannot be hidden. Neither do people light a lamp and put it under a bowl. Instead they put it on its stand, and it gives light to everyone in the house. In the same way, let your light shine before others, that they may see your good deeds and glorify your Father in heaven" (Matthew 5:14–16).

Our "lights" are our good works, or good deeds, that are intended to glorify God. If we are to be justice seekers, we need to show up with this light, especially in the dark times. In fact, Jesus says we should put our "lamps" on display, just as people of his day put their lamps on a stand. This way, the light from the lamp illuminated a large area. In spite of the darkness, the light would shine and expose what was hidden in the dark (see 1 Corinthians 4:5).

Without our light, the world will remain dark. Evil and injustice will remain hidden in the shadows. People will not be able to see until we place our lamps on a stand and shine it brightly. For this reason, we need to fight against the temptation to give up and not allow ourselves to be pulled down into despair. We must never succumb to the hopelessness, apathy, and silence around us. Instead, we must choose to let our light "shine before others."

9 The true light that gives light to everyone was coming into the world. 10 He was in the world, and though the world was made through him, the world did not recognize him. 11 He came to that which was his own, but his own did not receive him. 12 Yet to all who did receive him, to those who believed in his name, he gave the right to become children of God— 13 children born not of natural descent, nor of human decision or a husband's will, but born of God (John 1:9–13).

1. John opens his Gospel with this statement on how Jesus brought God's light into the world. How did some of the people of the time respond to that light? What did those who chose to recognize the light of Christ and believe in his name receive from God?

When Jesus spoke again to the people, he said, "I am the light of the world. Whoever follows me will never walk in darkness, but will have the light of life" (John 8:12).

2. How is Jesus the light of the world? What is the promise that Jesus gives for those who follow him?

3. How can the good deeds you do for God's glory be seen as a light in the midst of the darkness in our world? How have you seen light from others' good deeds?

4. How can we step into others' dark nights? What messages do our actions reveal as we provide light in a dark world?

5. How was Dr. King a light in the midst of darkness of his times? What characteristics of his can you model? What actions of Christ can you model to shed light in a dark world?

MOVE PAST THE DARKNESS

"Well, I don't know what will happen now. We've got some difficult days ahead. But it doesn't matter with me now. Because I've been to the mountaintop. And I don't mind. Like anybody, I would like to live a long life. Longevity has its place. But I'm not concerned about that now. I just want to do God's will."[32] Dr. King spoke these words on April 3, 1968, in Memphis, Tennessee. The next day, he was killed by an assassin's bullet.

The country was indeed in a dark place. Jim Crow laws were keeping people separate based on the color of their skin. Discrimination prohibited children of color from equal access to a quality education. Hate-induced violence permeated the land. Yet in the midst of these conditions—in the midst of the terror done to his own people—Dr. King could say he had "been to the mountaintop." He had hope informed by his view of God and his understanding of God's purpose for humanity.

Today, the list of ills in our country is just as long as they were in the civil rights movement. Injustice still exists. Children still do not have access to a quality education. Laws still unjustly target people of color. These circumstances create a dark world, and we have even more difficult days ahead. But as followers of Jesus, we have been to the mountaintop. We have hope in Christ . . . and that empowers us to continue to do God's will.

> ² How long, Lord, must I call for help,
>   but you do not listen?
> Or cry out to you, "Violence!"
>   but you do not save?
> Why do you make me look at injustice?
>   Why do you tolerate wrongdoing?
> Destruction and violence are before me;
>   there is strife, and conflict abounds.

A Path Upward

People are often surprised to learn that I am an optimist. They know how often I have been jailed, how frequently the days and nights have been filled with frustration and sorrow, how bitter and dangerous are my adversaries. They expect these experiences to harden me into a grim and desperate man. They fail, however, to perceive the sense of affirmation generated by the challenge of embracing struggle and surmounting obstacles. They have no comprehension of the strength that comes from faith in God and man.

It is possible for me to falter, but I am profoundly secure in my knowledge that God loves us; he has not worked out a design for our failure. Man has the capacity to do right as well as wrong, and his history is a path upward, not downward. The past is strewn with the ruins of the empires of tyranny, and each is a monument not merely to man's blunders but to his capacity to overcome them. . . . Millions of people have fought thousands of battles to enlarge my freedom; restricted as it still is, progress has been made. This is why I remain an optimist, though I am also a realist, about the barriers before us. . . .

A voice out of Bethlehem two thousand years ago said that all men are equal. It said right would triumph. Jesus of Nazareth wrote no books; he owned no property to endow him with influence. He had no friends in the courts of the powerful. But he changed the course of mankind with only the poor and the despised. Naïve and unsophisticated though we may be, the poor and despised of the twentieth century will revolutionize this era.

DR. MARTIN LUTHER KING JR.

FROM "A TESTAMENT OF HOPE," THE LAST ESSAY
WRITTEN BY DR. KING, PUBLISHED AFTER HIS DEATH[33]

> 4 Therefore the law is paralyzed,
>   and justice never prevails.
> The wicked hem in the righteous,
>   so that justice is perverted (Habakkuk 1:2–4).

1. The prophet Habakkuk penned these words as he witnessed the nation of Judah descend ever deeper into violence, injustice, and idolatry. How does he feel as he cries out to God? What specifically does he ask God to do in the situation?

2. Use the prophet's words to write your own lament. What do you want to ask God about the injustices you see in the world today—and what do you want him to do?

> 16 Yet I will wait patiently for the day of calamity
>   to come on the nation invading us.
> 17 Though the fig tree does not bud
>   and there are no grapes on the vines,
> though the olive crop fails
>   and the fields produce no food,
> though there are no sheep in the pen
>   and no cattle in the stalls,
> 18 yet I will rejoice in the LORD,
>   I will be joyful in God my Savior (Habakkuk 3:16–18).

3. Habakkuk understood that the situation in Judah would not remain the same forever. A day was coming when the people would reap what they had sown. This ultimately came in the form of the Babylonian captivity, when the nation was invaded and its people taken into exile. Even considering this outcome, what hope did Habakkuk express for God's people?

4. How can this confident hope in God inspire you as you wait on him and work for justice?

5. "Rejoice in the Lord always. I will say it again: Rejoice!" (Philippians 4:4). How will you rejoice in God as you wait—even knowing there are difficult days ahead?

CONNECT & CATCH UP

Take time today to connect with a fellow group member and discuss the key insights from this session. Use any of the following prompts to help guide your discussion.

What is the biblical definition of hope?

How has your understanding of hope been affirmed or challenged?

How will hope in God inspire you to keep working and taking steps for justice when things seem dark?

What particular passages of Scripture remind you to hope in God?

Use this time to go back and complete any of the study and reflection questions from previous days that you weren't able to finish. Make a note below of any revelations you've had and reflect on any growth or personal insights you've gained. Talk with your group about what study you want to go through next. Put a date on the calendar for when you will next meet to study God's Word and dive deeper into community.

LEADER'S GUIDE

Thank you for your willingness to lead your group through this study! What you have chosen to do is valuable and will make a great difference in the lives of others. *Share the Dream* is a six-session Bible study built around video content and small-group interaction. As the group leader, imagine yourself as the host of a party. Your job is to take care of your guests by managing the details so that when your guests arrive, they can focus on one another and on the interaction around the topic for that session.

Your role as the group leader is not to answer all the questions or reteach the content—the video and study guide will do most of that work. Your job is to guide the experience and cultivate your small group into a connected and engaged community. This will make it a place for members to process, question, and reflect.

There are several elements in this leader's guide that will help you as you structure your study and reflection time, so be sure to follow along and take advantage of each one.

BEFORE YOU BEGIN

Before your first meeting, make sure the group members have a copy of this study guide. Alternatively, you can hand out the study guides at your first meeting and give the members some time to look over the material and ask any preliminary questions. Also make sure they are aware that they have access to the streaming videos at any time. During your first meeting, ask the members to provide their name, phone number, and email address so you can keep in touch with them.

Generally, the ideal size for a group is eight to ten people, which will ensure that everyone has enough time to participate in discussions. If you have more people, you might want to break up the main group into smaller subgroups. Encourage those who show up at the first meeting to commit to attending the duration of the study, as this will help the group members get to know one another, create stability for the group, and help you know how to best prepare to lead them through the material.

Each of the sessions begins with an opening reflection in the Welcome section. The questions that follow in the Connect section serve as an icebreaker to get the group members thinking about the topic. Some people may want to tell a long story in response to one of these questions, but the goal is to keep the answers brief. Ideally, you want everyone in the group to get a chance to answer, so try to keep the responses to a minute or less. If you have talkative group members, say up front that everyone needs to be brief so that everyone has time to share.

Give the group members a chance to answer, but also tell them to feel free to pass if they wish. With the rest of the study, it's generally best not to have everyone answer every question—a free-flowing discussion is more desirable. But with the opening icebreaker questions, you can go around the circle.

At your first meeting, let the group members know that each session contains a personal study section they can use to continue to engage with the content. While this is optional, it will help them cement the concepts presented during the group study time. Invite them to bring any questions and insights to your next meeting, especially if they had a breakthrough moment or didn't understand something.

PREPARATION FOR EACH SESSION

As the leader, there are a few things you should do to prepare for each meeting:

- **Read through the session.** This will help you become more familiar with the content and know how to structure the discussion times.

- **Decide how the videos will be used.** Determine whether you want the members to watch the videos ahead of time or together as a group.

- **Decide which questions you want to discuss.** Based on the length of your group discussions, you may not be able to get through all the questions. So look over the questions and choose which ones you definitely want to cover.

- **Be familiar with the questions you want to discuss.** When the group meets you'll be watching the clock, so make sure you are familiar with the questions that you have selected. In this way, you will ensure that you have the material more deeply in your mind than your group members.

- **Pray for your group.** Pray for your group members and ask God to lead them as they study his Word.

Note that in most cases, there won't be a "right" answer to the question. Answers will vary, especially when members are being asked to share their personal experiences.

STRUCTURING THE DISCUSSION TIME

You will need to determine how long you want to meet so you can plan your time accordingly. Suggested times for each section have been provided in this study guide, and if you adhere to these times, your group will meet for ninety minutes. If you want to meet for two hours, follow the times given in the right-hand column:

Section	90 Minutes	120 Minutes
CONNECT (discuss one or more of the opening questions for the session)	15 minutes	20 minutes
WATCH (watch the teaching material together and take notes)	20 minutes	20 minutes
DISCUSS (discuss the study questions you selected ahead of time)	35 minutes	50 minutes
RESPOND (write down key takeaways)	10 minutes	15 minutes
PRAY (pray together and dismiss)	10 minutes	15 minutes

As the group leader, it is up to you to keep track of the time and stay on schedule. You might want to set a timer for each segment so both you and the group members know when your time is up. (There are some good phone apps for timers that play a gentle chime or other upbeat sounds instead of a disruptive noise.)

Don't be concerned if the group members are quiet or slow to share. People are often quiet when they are pulling together their ideas, and this might be a new experience for them. Just ask a question and let it hang in the air until someone shares. You can then say, "Thank you. What about others? What came to you when you watched that portion of the teaching?"

GROUP DYNAMICS

Leading a group through *Share the Dream* will be rewarding to you and your group members. But you still may encounter challenges along the way! Discussions can get off track. Group members may not be sensitive to the needs and ideas of others. Some might worry they will be expected to talk about matters that make them feel awkward. Others may express comments that result in disagreements. To help ease this strain on you and the group, consider the following ground rules:

- When someone raises a question or comment that is off the main topic, suggest that you deal with it another time, or, if you feel led to go in that direction, let the group know you will be spending some time discussing it.

- If someone asks a question that you don't know how to answer, admit it and move on. At your discretion, feel free to invite group members to comment on questions that call for personal experience.

- If you find one or two people are dominating the discussion time, direct a few questions to others in the group. Outside the main group time, ask the more dominating members to help you draw out the quieter ones. Work to make them a part of the solution instead of part of the problem.

- When a disagreement occurs, encourage the group members to process the matter in love. Encourage those on opposite sides to restate what they heard the other side say about the matter, and then invite each side to evaluate if that perception is accurate. Lead the group in examining other scriptures related to the topic and look for common ground.

When these issues arise, encourage your group members to follow these words from Scripture: "Love one another" (John 13:34), "If it is possible, as far as it depends on you, live at peace with everyone" (Romans 12:18), "Whatever is true . . . noble . . . right . . . if anything is excellent or praiseworthy—think about such things" (Philippians 4:8), and "Be quick to listen, slow to speak and slow to become angry" (James 1:19). This will make your group time more rewarding and beneficial for everyone who attends.

Thank you again for leading your group. You are making a difference in your members' lives and having an impact as they learn to embrace the biblical concepts of *love, conscience, justice, freedom, perseverance,* and *hope* and *share the dream.*

ABOUT THE AUTHORS

Chris Broussard, a longtime journalist, NBA analyst, and sports broadcaster, serves as cohost of FS1's *First Things First* television show and Fox Sports Radio's *The Odd Couple*. Broussard rose to national prominence as an NBA reporter at the *New York Times*, where he covered the NBA at large from 1998 to 2004. He is involved in numerous charitable endeavors, including serving as founder and president of The K.I.N.G. Movement.

Matthew Daniels JD, PhD, is the Chair of Law & Human Rights at the Institute of World Politics in Washington, DC, where he focuses on countering violent extremist ideologies through education. He collaborated with Ambassador Andrew Young and colleagues from several historically black colleges to create K12 curricula teaching Dr. King's nonviolent principles to a digital generation. He is also the founder of Good of All, an educational non-profit which in 2019 launched an Andrew Young HBCU Scholarship program in partnership with the Thurgood Marshall College Fund.

ENDNOTES

1. Drew Hansen, *The Dream: Martin Luther King Jr. and the Speech That Inspired a Nation* (New York: HarperCollins, 2003), 177.

2. Taylor Branch, *Parting the Waters: America in the King Years, 1954–1963* (New York: Simon & Schuster, 2006).

3. "I Have a Dream," Wikipedia, https://en.wikipedia.org/wiki/I_Have_a_Dream#cite_ref-7.

4. Jon Meacham, "One Man," *Time,* August 26, 2013, 26.

5. Dr. Martin Luther King Jr., from "I See the Promised Land," sermon delivered at the Bishop Charles Mason Temple in Memphis, Tennessee, on April 3, 1968. Taken from James M. Washington, editor, *A Testament of Hope: The Essential Writings and Speeches of Martin Luther King Jr.* (San Francisco, CA: HarperOne, 1986), 284–285.

6. Dr. Martin Luther King Jr., *The Strength to Love* (Minneapolis, MN: Fortress Press, 1982), 153

7. Lucas Morel and Constance Murray, "Martin Luther King Publishes His Letter from a Birmingham Jail," EDSITEment, National Endowment for the Humanities, November 13, 2009, https://edsitement.neh.gov/this-day/martin-luther-king-publishes-his-letter-birmingham jail#:~:text=King%20wrote%20his%22Letter%20from,streets%20to%20secure%20civil%20rights.

8. Dr. Martin Luther King Jr., from "Letter from Birmingham City Jail," open letter to eight clergymen, written April 16, 1963, from a jail in Birmingham, Alabama. Taken from Washington, *A Testament of Hope*, 297.

9. Dr. Martin Luther King Jr., from "A Strength to Love," a collection of sermons delivered at the Ebenezer Baptist Church in Atlanta, Georgia, and elsewhere, which was first published in 1963. Taken from Washington, *A Testament of Hope*, 494–495.

10. Bishop Todd Hunter, "2's Day: Jesus and MLK," The Center for Formation Justice and Peace, https://centerfjp.org/article-posts/2s-day-jesus-and-mlk/.

11. Dr. Martin Luther King Jr., from an undated interview with Dr. Kenneth B. Clark, a noted child psychologist and educator. Taken from Washington, *A Testament of Hope*, 334–335.

12. "Vietnam War," The Martin Luther King Jr. Research and Education Institute, Stanford University, https://kinginstitute.stanford.edu/encyclopedia/vietnam-war#:~:text=King%20delivered%20a%20speech%20entitled,Harlem%E2%80%9D%20(King%2C%20%E2%80%9CBeyond.

13. Dr. Martin Luther King Jr., from the sermon "Conscience and the Vietnam War," aired by the Canadian Broadcasting Corporation, November–December 1967, as part of the seventh annual Massey Lectures, named after the former governor general of Canada. Taken from Washington, *A Testament of Hope,* 634, 639.

14. Dr. Martin Luther King Jr., from "A Time to Break Silence," address at meeting of Clergy and Laity Concerned, Riverside Church in New York City, April 4, 1967. Taken from Washington, *A Testament of Hope,* 243

15. "Baptist Street Church Bombing," History: Famous Cases & Criminals, FTB, https://www.fbi.gov/history/famous-cases/baptist-street-church-bombing.

16. Dr. Martin Luther King Jr., "Death of Illusions," The Martin Luther King Jr. Research and Education Institute, Stanford University, https://kinginstitute.stanford.edu/chapter-21-death-illusions#:~:text=We%20must%20not%20become%20bitter,worth%20of%20all%20human%20personality.

17. "Substitute Courage for Caution: MLK's 'Eulogy' and the Charleston Church Shooting," June 19, 2015, https://www.beaconbroadside.com/broadside/2015/06/substitute-courage-for-caution.html

18. Dr. Martin Luther King Jr., from "Showdown for Nonviolence," an article published in *Look* magazine on April 16, 1968, two weeks after Dr. King was assassinated in Memphis, Tennessee, on April 4, 1968. Taken from Washington, *A Testament of Hope*, 69.

19. Dr. Martin Luther King Jr., from "Love, Law, and Civil Disobedience," a transcription of an address before the annual meeting of the Fellowship of the Concerned, which took place on November 16, 1961. Taken from Washington, *A Testament of Hope,* 48–49.

20. "Rosa Parks," History.com, January 11, 2023, https://www.history.com/topics/black-history/rosa-parks.

21. Dr. Martin Luther King Jr., "Letter from Birmingham City Jail," taken from Washington, *A Testament of Hope*, 292.

22. Dr. Martin Luther King Jr., "The Birth of a New Nation," sermon delivered at Dexter Avenue Baptist Church in Montgomery, Alabama, on April 7, 1957, https://kinginstitute.stanford.edu/king-papers/documents/birth-new-nation-sermon-delivered-dexter-avenue-baptist-church#ftnref1.

23. Dr. Martin Luther King Jr., from "The Ethical Demands for Integration," speech delivered at a church conference in Nashville, Tennessee, on December 27, 1962. Taken from Washington, *A Testament of Hope,* 120.

24. Eugene H. Peterson, *The Message* (Colorado Spring, CO: NavPress, 1993, 2002, 2018), translation of Matthew 11:30.

25. Dr. Martin Luther King Jr., from "An Address Before the National Press Club," delivered in Washington, DC, on July 19, 1962. Taken from Washington, *A Testament of Hope,* 104–105.

26. Dr. Martin Luther King Jr., "Why Jesus Called a Man a Fool," sermon delivered at Mount Pisgah Missionary Baptist Church, Chicago, Illinois, on August 27, 1967.

27. Adam Hosey, "MLK Day Reflections: Learning from Setbacks Builds Resilience for Success (opinion)," One United Lancaster, January 17, 2022, https://oneunitedlancaster.com/community-voices-coronavirus/mlk-day-reflections-learning-from-setbacks-builds-resilience-for-success-opinion/; Samuel Momodu, "The Albany Movement," Black Past, August 31, 2016. https://www.blackpast.org/african-american-history/albany-movement-1961-1962/.

28. Holly Lebowitz Rossi, "Martin Luther King Jr. on 'Infinite Hope,'" Guideposts, https://guideposts.org/inspiring-stories/stories-of-faith-and-hope/martin-luther-king-jr-on-infinite-hope/.

29. Dr. Martin Luther King Jr., from *Stride Toward Freedom: The Montgomery Story*, a memoir by Dr. King about the Montgomery bus boycott that took place from December 5, 1955, to December 20, 1956. Dr. King wrote the book with the help of scholars such as George D. Kelsey and Lawrence D. Reddick. It was published by Harper & Brothers on September 17, 1958. Taken from Washington, *A Testament of Hope*, 482.

30. Dr. Martin Luther King Jr., from "Facing the Challenge of a New Age," an address given at the First Annual Institute on Non-Violence and Social Change, held in Montgomery, Alabama, in December 1956. Taken from Washington, *A Testament of Hope*, 141–143.

31. Dr. Martin Luther King Jr., from *Where Do We Go from Here: Chaos or Community?*, published by Beacon Press in 1967. The book—the fourth by Dr. King and the final one published before his death in 1968—was written in the midst of a grueling schedule and was perhaps the toughest writing project that he ever pursued. Dr. King finally had to travel to an isolated residence in Jamaica, with no telephone, to complete it. Taken from Washington, *A Testament of Hope*, 632.

32. Dr. Martin Luther King Jr., "I've Been to the Mountaintop," speech given in support of the striking sanitation workers at Mason Temple in Memphis, Tennessee, on April 3, 1968, https://www.afscme.org/about/history/mlk/mountaintop

33. Dr. Martin Luther King Jr., from "A Testament of Hope," written before his assassination on April 4, 1968, and published posthumously in 1969. Taken from Washington, *A Testament of Hope*, 314, 328.